Brain Power

Flight

Penny Clarke

BOOK HOUSE

Contents

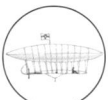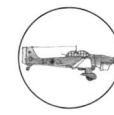

FLIGHTS OF FANCY

When did humans first want to fly? Who knows? But it's easy to understand why they wanted to. Birds make it look so easy, darting after prey and flying over obstacles like forests and rivers. Many insects do the same. But birds have a huge number of muscles in their wings, so humans faced a problem. Compared with birds, our bodies are too heavy to be lifted by our arm muscles.

Fly like birds?

Birds do not fly just by flapping their wings, but it was millions of years before humans discovered that. Now we know that humans will never be able to fly in the same way as birds.

First parachute?

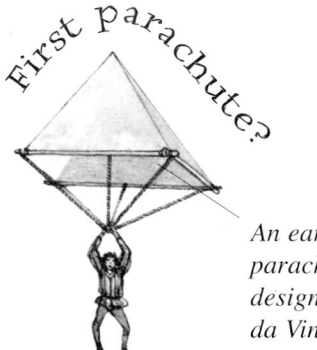

An early parachute designed by da Vinci

Leonardo da Vinci, the great Italian artist and scientist, designed the first-known helicopters and parachutes. He drew the parachute above in about 1500, but it was never built.

Famous Flyer
Oliver of Malmesbury
11th century

whisssh

That didn't work!

Who was Oliver of Malmesbury?

Oliver of Malmesbury (left), an English monk who lived in the eleventh century, was determined to fly. He attached home-made feathered wings to his arms. Legend says he 'flew' 180 metres although this is doubtful, but like all bird men, he eventually crashed back down to Earth.

Birds as gods!

It's not surprising early people worshipped birds as gods. The way eagles, for example, soar upwards hardly moving their wings seems miraculous. People did not know that birds used 'thermals' (currents of hot air), to carry them. This winged god (above) was drawn on an ancient Egyptian tomb about 5,000 years ago. People in South America, Persia, China and Rome also worshipped winged gods.

Flying kings?

According to legend, in 1500 BC King Kai Kawus of Persia (modern Iran) harnessed four geese to his throne. Did they really lift king and throne as shown to the left?

Is it an eagle?

An artefact showing a fierce winged god from ancient Mexico (below). Perhaps it represents a bird like an eagle.

Mexican artefact

Wings of feather and wax!

Icarus

Daedalus

By closely observing how birds fly, Leonardo da Vinci realised human arms were too weak for flight. He designed about 150 flying machines using levers and pulleys to give the arm muscles greater strength.

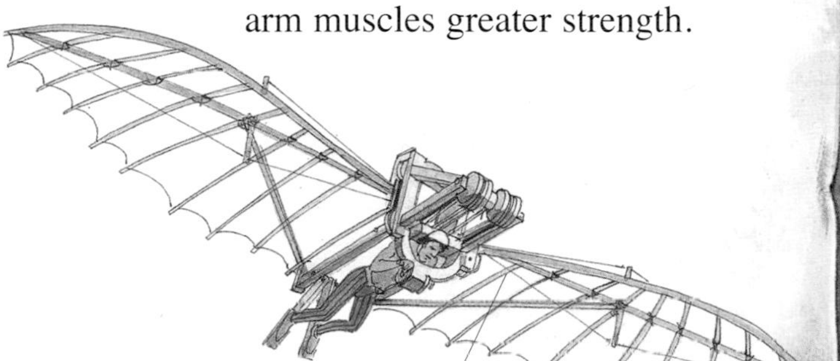

In Greek legend King Minos of Crete imprisoned Daedalus and his son Icarus. They escaped by making wings of feathers and wax. Daedalus warned Icarus against flying near the sun because the wax would melt. Icarus disobeyed (above), the wax melted and he drowned.

One of da Vinci's designs for a flying machine. It would have been too heavy to ever fly.

FIRST BALLOON FLIGHTS

Despite Leonardo's genius, human flight remained a dream. But inventors did not give up, they just looked for other ways to lift humans off the ground. Hot air seemed promising. In June 1783 Joseph (left) and Etienne Montgolfier used hot air and a paper-lined linen bag 11 metres in diameter, and it rose to 1,800 metres. But balloons using hot air had to be huge to lift useful weights. Hydrogen, a gas discovered in 1766 by the English chemist Henry Cavendish, seemed a better possibility.

Famous Flyer
Marquis d'Arlandes

Au revoir!

Crew: a cockerel a duck and a sheep!

In September 1783 came the first 'manned' balloon flight. The crew were a cockerel, a duck and a sheep!

Marquis d'Arlandes on his famous flight

Highly flammable!

The Montgolfiers' successful experiment encouraged others. In November 1783 the Marquis d'Arlandes and a companion flew 9 kilometres across Paris in a hot-air balloon. Early ballooning was very dangerous. To make the hot air to power the balloon, a burning brazier hung just below the balloon which was made of highly flammable material.

Professor Jacques Charles used hydrogen in a balloon in 1783 – a first!

Gas balloon!

In 1837 Sir George Cayley designed an airship with a streamlined gas balloon (below). It was not built.

In 1791 André Jacques Garnerin astonished Parisians, descending by parachute (above) from his balloon.

Everything overboard!

In 1785 American John Jeffries, and Frenchman Jean-Pierre Blanchard made the first balloon flight across the English Channel. It was almost a disaster because the balloon leaked. However, because they threw everything possible overboard they landed safely in a forest near Calais.

Clockwork!

Pierre Jullien followed George Cayley's ideas about streamlining. His model airship (right), made in 1850, had a clockwork-driven propeller.

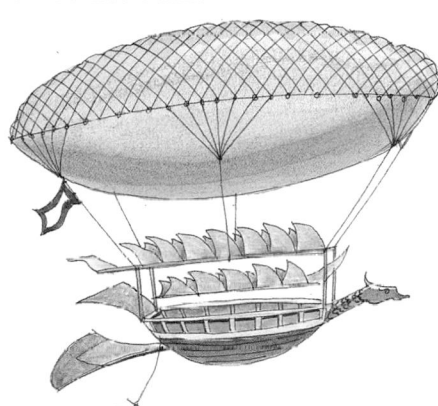

Streamlined airship!

In 1852 Henri Giffard, a French engineer, proved that streamlining really worked. His airship (below left), with a streamlined hydrogen-filled bag and steam engine to turn a propeller, carried him from Paris to Trappes, a distance of 27 kilometres.

Electric powered balloon!

In 1884, only 101 years after the first balloon flight, came *La France* (below). Electrically powered, its top speed was 22 km/h.

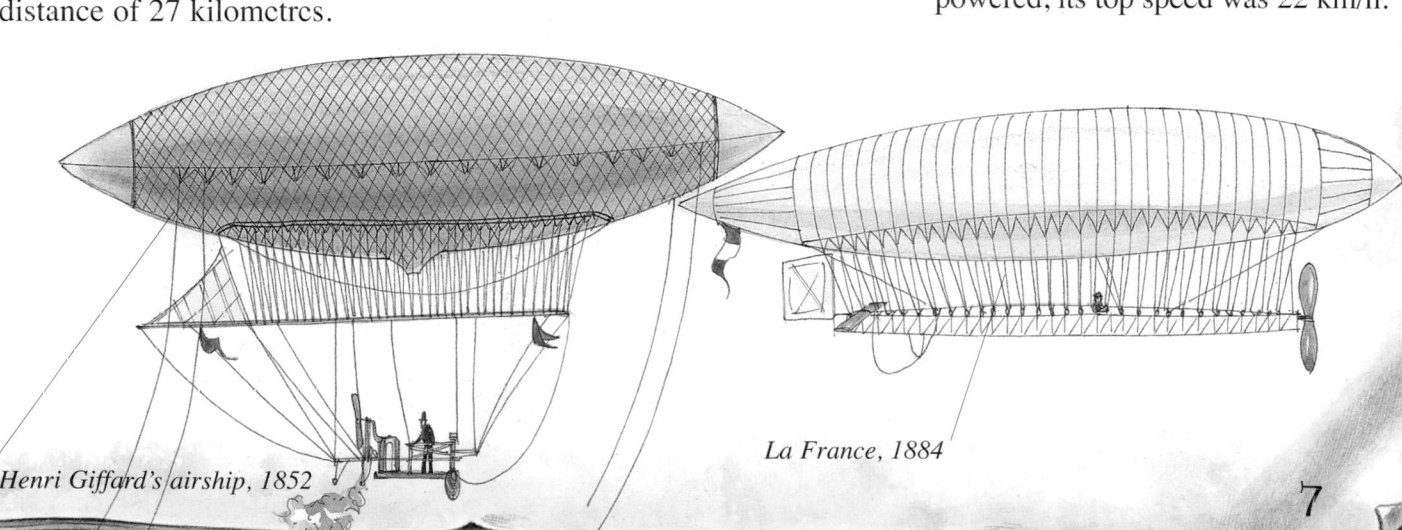

Henri Giffard's airship, 1852

La France, 1884

KITES AND GLIDERS

Balloons and early airships had one enormous drawback: they were completely at the mercy of the wind. In 1804, the engineer Sir George Cayley built a model glider. From this model came the aircraft and flying as we know today. Not content with models, he made ever bigger gliders, ending with a manned glider in 1853. Others built on his work, including the German, Otto Lilienthal. He developed gliders very like today's hang-gliders, but died when one crashed. What gliders now needed were engines.

1804...

Almost 50 years separate Cayley's model glider of 1804 (above) and his final one of 1853 (below). But both had fixed wings and a moveable tailplane – just like modern aircraft.

...nearly fifty years later!

Cayley's glider, 1853

Famous Flyer
Otto Lilienthal's
Glide Flyer 1893

Squawk!

In 1893 Otto Lilienthal made the first truly controlled flight and glided a distance of up to 230 metres.

8

Passenger carrying kites!

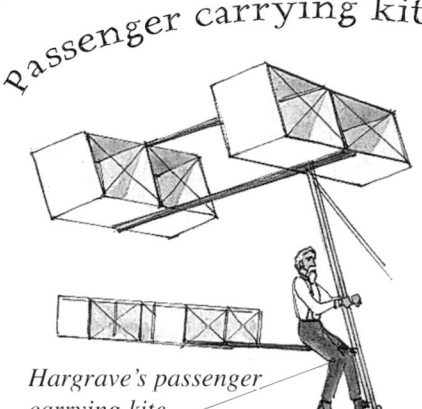

Hargrave's passenger carrying kite

In Australia in the 1890s Lawrence Hargrave designed and developed several people-carrying kites (above). His kites had box-like wings and flew well. He discovered that they flew even better if the surfaces of the wings were curved on top. This shape, the airfoil, gives the greatest lift. Many of the first aircraft used similar wing and tail designs.

Flying author!

Octave Chanute was a leading American builder of kites. As well as testing his designs (right), he wrote a book describing his work.

Octave Chanute

A box kite!

In 1893 Lawrence Hargrave designed the box kite (left). The following year it lifted him 5 metres off the ground.

Lawrence Hargrave's box kite

Military kite!

In America Samuel Cody realised just how useful passenger-carrying kites would be for military use. In 1904 he produced a type of box kite. From it hung a basket in which the passenger sat with a gun, camera, telescope and telephone (below).

Scottish glider!

The Scottish engineer Percy Pilcher designed and built some very successful hang-gliders, including the Hawk (left). Unfortunately he died when it crashed in 1899.

Like the birds . . .

Like Leonardo da Vinci 500 years earlier (page 4), Wilbur Wright noticed that when a bird glides, it twists the tips of its wings to control its direction and speed.

Wilbur tried to use this observation in the gliders he and his brother, Orville, were developing at their home in Dayton, in the US. In 1902 and 1903 the two brothers made hundreds of successful flights in their gliders.

One of the Wright brothers' glider experiments

Samuel Cody's passenger-carrying kite

9

IS THIS REALLY FLYING?

In 1712 the first practical steam engine was built by the English engineer Thomas Newcomen. The world's first railway, the Stockton and Darlington, opened in 1825 with George Stephenson's steam locomotives pulling the trains. But gliders must be light to become airborne and these early engines were heavy. The designers knew this, but steam was the best power source available so they experimented with it.

Model aircraft!

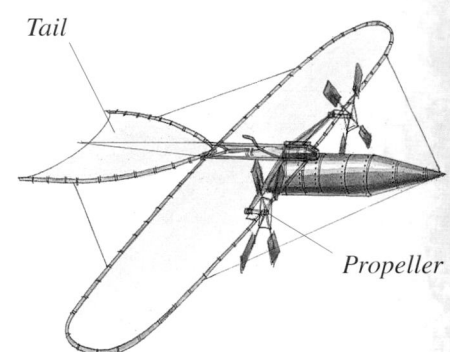

Tail

Propeller

Model aircraft were used for many flying experiments. In 1879 Victor Tatin of France used compressed air to power his model.

Famous 'non'-flyer
Samuel Langley's Aerodrome!
1903

Catapult launch!

In 1896 Professor Samuel P. Langley's steam-powered model aircraft flew for almost a kilometre. From this he developed Aerodrome, the first full-sized aircraft to fly with a petrol engine. Launched by catapult from a houseboat on the Potomac River, USA in 1903, it was too heavy and crashed. Langley was widely ridiculed in the press and abandoned his dream of flying after this failure.

Too heavy to fly!

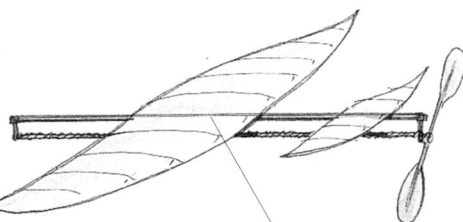

Aerial steam carriage

The Aerial Steam Carriage, designed by William Henson in 1843, was ahead of its time. In theory it could fly, but in practice the engines of this time were so heavy that it could not!

Twisted rubber band!

Alphonse Pénaud's model plane *Planophore* (1871) was powered by a twisted rubber band.

Planophore

Steam powered aircraft...

In 1874 Félix du Temple's steam-powered machine ran down a ramp called a 'hop' and stayed airborne for only a few seconds. This was lucky as he had no way of controlling it in the air.

Félix du Temple's steam-powered aircraft

...but could they fly?

In Russia in 1884, Alexander Mozhaisky tested his steam-powered plane (below). It also 'flew' after running down a ramp.

Of all these pioneers the French engineer Clément Ader came closest to flying with his bat-winged *Eole*.

In 1890 with a very light steam engine Ader kept *Eole* airborne (in fact only 20 centimetres off the ground) for 150 metres.

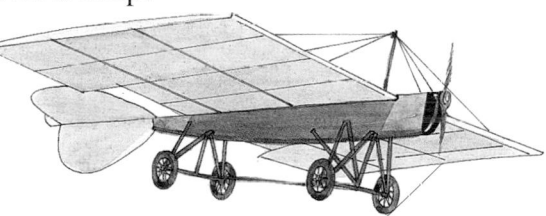

Broad wings over the whole length of body

Bat-wings

Eole

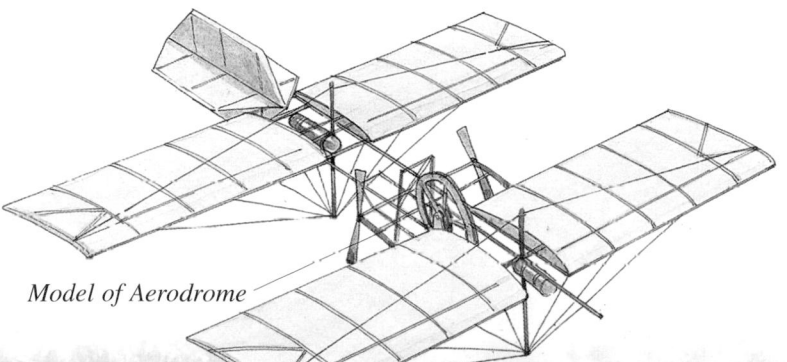

Model of Aerodrome

Before building the full-size *Aerodrome*, Langley built a 1/4 size model. During test flights, this model flew without problems which then gave him the confidence to continue work on a full-size version. Sadly, his success with the model was not repeated in the final *Aerodrome* (see opposite).

FLYER IS AIRBORNE!

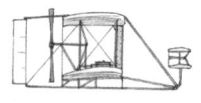

On 17 December 1903 two American brothers who made bicycles for a living finally proved to the world that humans could fly! They were ignored at first because just before their success, Professor Langley's attempt with *Aerodrome* had failed (page 10). Orville and Wilbur Wright succeeded because they could control their aircraft, *Flyer* (above). Before that everyone, including Langley, had focused on getting airborne and had not thought about what they would do once they got there.

Flying gliders!

Their experience of flying gliders (as shown above) helped the Wrights to make successful aircraft.

Flyer *became airborne at Kitty Hawk, North Carolina, on 17 December 1903. In 12 seconds it reached 3 metres in altitude and travelled about 36 metres. Before taking off,* Flyer *ran along a launch rail. It had two rear propellers to drive it forward and was controlled by twisting the main wings and adjusting the rear rudders. So began the modern age of flight.*

Famous Flight

Flyer takes off!

17 December 1903

We did it!

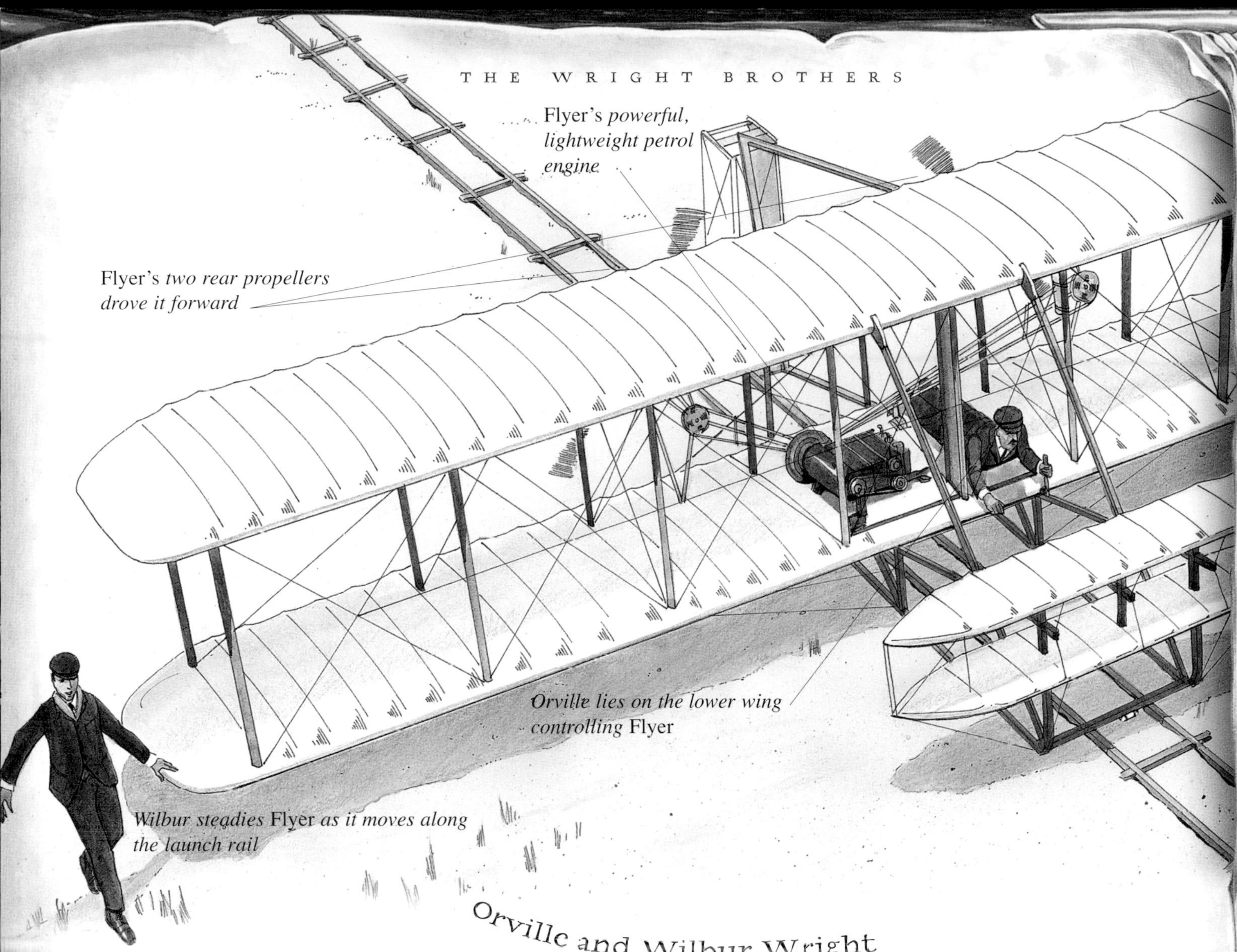

Flyer's *powerful, lightweight petrol engine*

Flyer's *two rear propellers drove it forward*

Orville lies on the lower wing controlling Flyer

Wilbur steadies Flyer *as it moves along the launch rail*

Orville and Wilbur Wright

Wind tunnel tests!

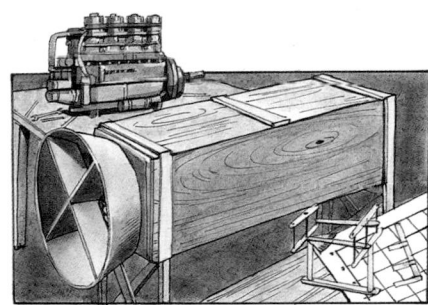

The brothers built a wind tunnel to test different wing shapes. They designed a light petrol engine, discovering it worked best if it turned faster than the propeller.

Orville Wright   *Wilbur Wright*

A toy helicopter, a present from their father, inspired the brothers' interest in flying. After the success of *Flyer* they went on making aircraft until Wilbur (above right) died of typhoid in 1912. Orville died in 1948, having seen the important part aircraft played in the Second World War.

Medals!

Ohio, the Wrights' home state, honoured their contribution to the world of aviation with these medals shown above.

13

PIONEERS OF THE AIR

After the Wrights' success, many different planes were produced. Some were more successful than others. Then, in 1909, six years after *Flyer* travelled just 36 metres, Louis Blériot took off from the French town of Calais aiming to reach England, 37 kilometres away across the English Channel. Blériot's success was marked with medals and merchandise, including the cigar box (above left).

A tin toy based on the plane Blériot successfully flew across the Channel. Blériot's plane was rarely more than a metre above the sea, but luckily it was calm!

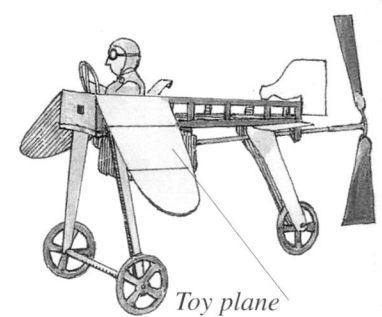

Toy plane

Famous Flight

Blériot crosses the Channel!

25 July 1909

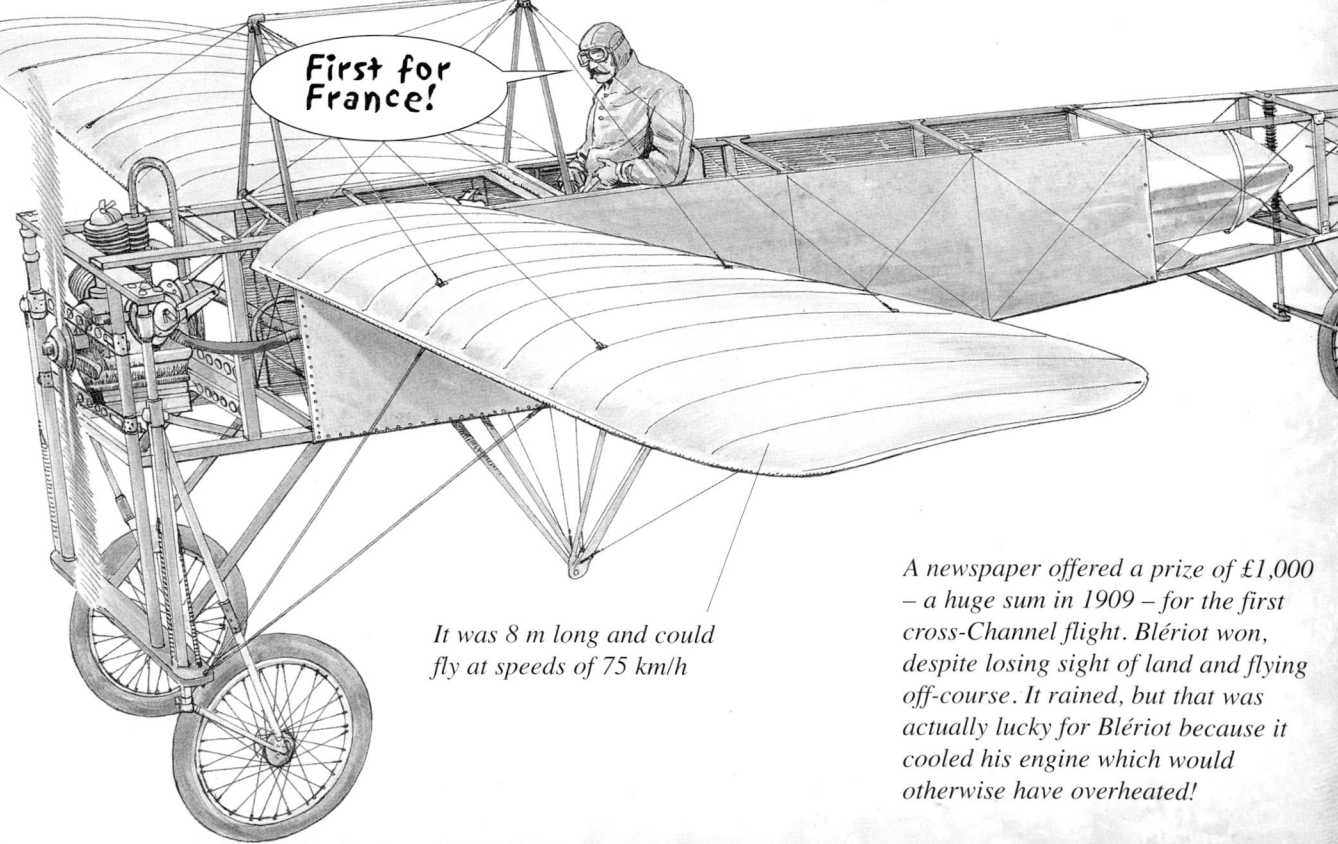

First for France!

It was 8 m long and could fly at speeds of 75 km/h

A newspaper offered a prize of £1,000 – a huge sum in 1909 – for the first cross-Channel flight. Blériot won, despite losing sight of land and flying off-course. It rained, but that was actually lucky for Blériot because it cooled his engine which would otherwise have overheated!

First to fly in Europe!

Santos-Dumont's 14-bis craft

In 1906, Brazilian millionaire, Alberto Santos-Dumont officially became the first person to fly in Europe and won the Deutsch-Archdeacon prize.

Early helicopter!

Early French helicopter

D.I.Y plane!

Demoiselle, the first 'build-it-yourself' plane, was designed and made by Santos-Dumont in 1907.

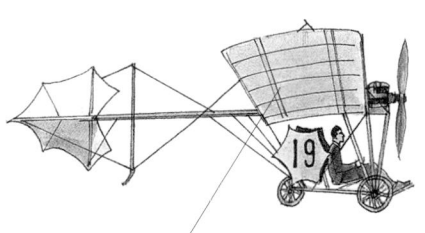

Demoiselle

As well as planes, engineers continued experimenting with helicopters. This twin-rotor machine (above) made by Paul Cornu, successfully made a short flight in 1907, but he could not afford to develop it.

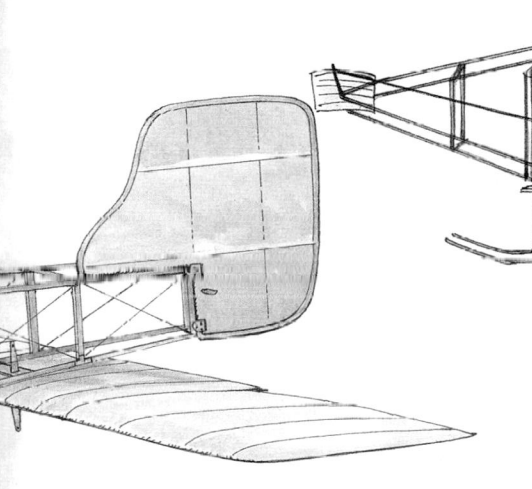

June Bug

In 1908 a biplane from Charles and Gabriel Voisin's aircraft factory (the world's first) flew in a circle of over a kilometre, winning them 50,000 francs.

Glenn Curtiss' *June Bug* flew almost 1.6 kilometres in 1908. This was later developed into the *Gold Bug*, which flew at Rheims in 1909.

Twin rotors!

Igor Sikorsky's 1909 helicopter (below) had two rotors. They turned in opposite directions, preventing the machine twisting in flight.

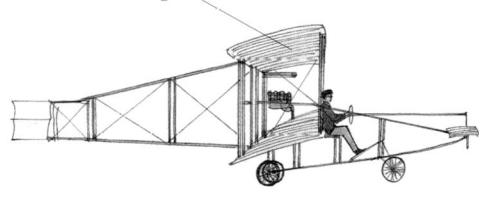

To save money, Roe covered it in brown paper

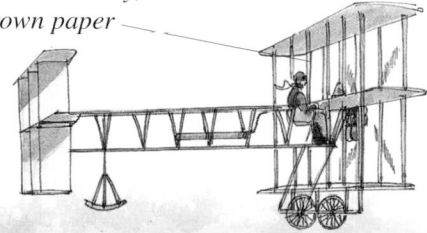

Brown paper plane!

A.V. Roe's triplane (three-winged plane) became the first successful British aircraft in 1909.

THE AVIATION CRAZE

The Wrights' success with *Flyer* inspired enormous interest in aviation, particularly in Europe. *Flyer* had rear propellers, but European aviators preferred designs with propellers at the front. Their planes also had better engines than American planes, because the European engine-making industry was more advanced. In August 1909, aircraft and pilots gathered at Rheims in France for the first air show. There were 38 planes and many flew over 4.8 kilometres – only six years after *Flyer*'s 36-metre-flight this was thought a triumph!

First mid-air collision over Milan 1910!

Whizzzzzzzz

Yikes!

Crunch!

Hubert Latham (above) was the first person to try for the £1,000 newspaper prize, but his plane crashed after only 3 kilometres. Six days after this failure, on 25 July 1909, Blériot made his successful flight.

Women also enjoyed flying, as the design on this fan shows

Fastest!

Blériot XII

The Wright's Flyer

Of all the planes at the Rheims air show, Blériot's *Blériot XII* was the fastest, reaching a speed of 76 km/h. Americans also competed at Rheims, but neither Glenn Curtiss's *Golden Flier* (below) nor the Wrights' *Flyer* (right) could match *Blériot XII's* speed.

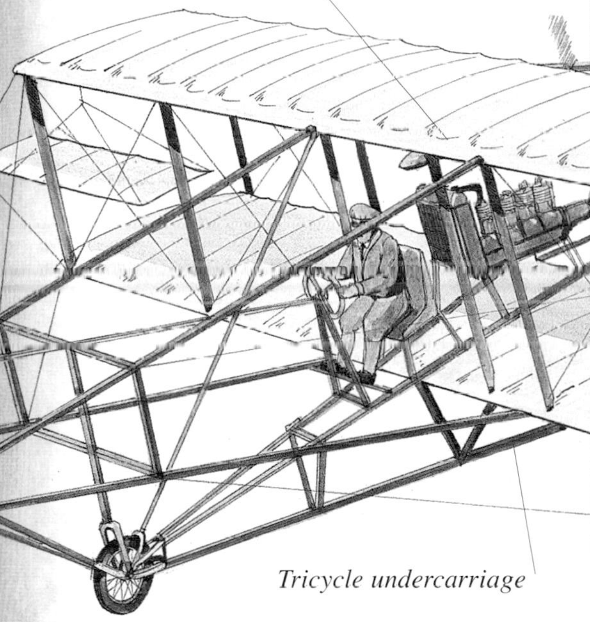

Golden Flier

Tricycle undercarriage

Ailerons between the wings

Another first: Louis Béchereau's 1913 Deperdussin racing plane (right) was the first plane to have a 'monocoque' fuselage. This means the frame supporting the plane's body is enclosed, making the plane much stronger.

The 1912 Avro F was the first monoplane with an enclosed cabin

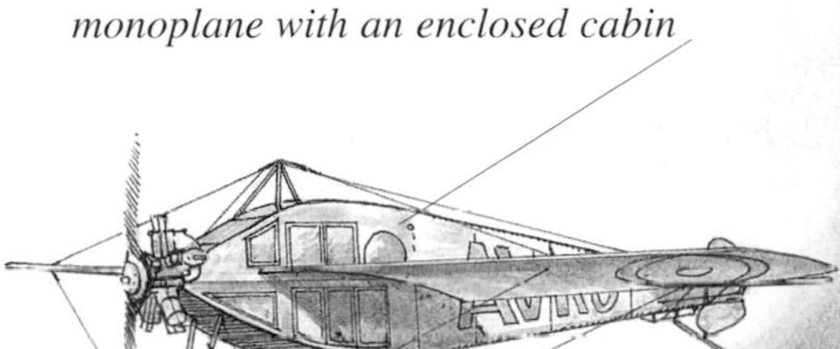

First enclosed cabin!

BOMBS AND BOMBERS

whoosh!

By 1910, the year after the Rheims air show, the political situation in Europe was becoming increasingly dangerous. The old empires of Austria-Hungary and Turkey were getting weaker, while Germany under Kaiser Wilhelm II, was becoming increasingly powerful. When World War I was declared in September 1914, military commanders quickly realised the usefulness of aircraft for gathering intelligence. When the war ended four years later, planes had become essential fighting machines. And every country realised it needed another efficient armed service: an airforce.

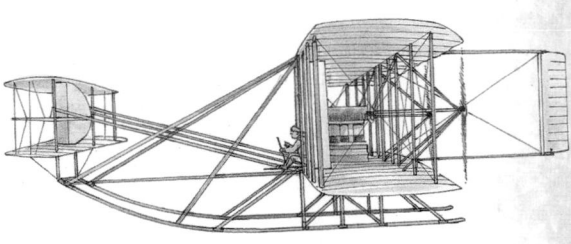

The two-seater Military Flyer *(above), developed by the Wrights in 1909, showed how planes could be used for military purposes. The extra seat was for an observer or a gunner.*

Wings of a dove!

Austrian Igo Etrich designed the *Taube* (German for 'dove') in 1910. Its almost translucent wings made it difficult to spot from the ground, but it was slow and difficult to manouevre which meant it was quickly outdated by new faster planes.

Famous Aviation Moment

Invention of the bomber!

1910

Bombs away!

Hands free!

The bird-like shape of the Taube *made it look rather old-fashioned, but it was an extremely stable plane. This allowed the pilot to take his hands off the controls and then there was nothing old-fashioned about the* Taube! *Its stability meant the pilot could throw out bombs and grenades, making it the world's first bomber with its first use in Libya in 1911. Sadly, the dove is traditionally a symbol of peace.*

18

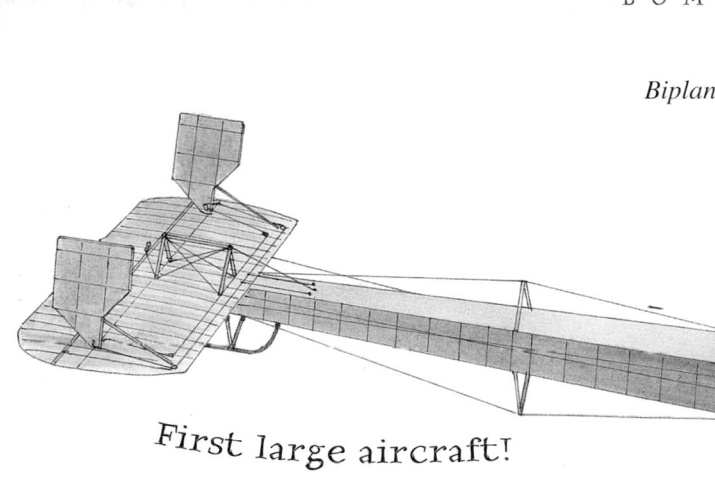

Biplane

Russkiy Vitiaz from 1913

First large aircraft!

As well as designing helicopters (page 15), the Russian engineer Igor Sikorsky also designed aircraft. His four-engine biplane, *Russkiy Vitiaz* ('Russian Knight'), was launched in May 1913 and was the world's first successful large aircraft. Its top speed was 97 km/h.

Does my head look big in this?

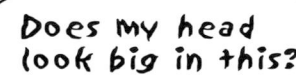

Goggles

B.S.1

The B.S.1 (*Blériot Scout 1*) was launched by Geoffrey de Havilland in 1913. Streamlined in shape, it had a top speed of 148 km/h.

High-flying fashions!

The first planes had open cockpits, so pilots needed warm, windproof clothing. At first, leather and sheepskin were the best materials. However by 1916 these were being replaced by waxed cotton lined with silk and fur. Helmets and goggles to protect the ears and eyes were also essential.

Sheepskin coat

Pilot wearing typical flying gear c.1910s

One of the first big bombers was the Italian built Caproni (left). Launched in 1915, it had a bomb load of 450 kilos. When flying over the Alps to attack Austrian targets the gunners stood for hours on open platforms in the bitter cold.

BATTLES IN THE AIR

A s the land armies continued to battle, aerial combat became important. At first pilots were only armed with revolvers, and then they took rifles. In two-seater planes (page 18) gunners used the second seat. Machine guns were soon added and pilots tried to shoot down as many enemy planes as possible. One of the most successful was German Manfred von Richthofen. He brought down 80 aircraft in 18 months before being killed. He was lucky, most pilots were shot down after only a few hours in the air.

The Fokker monoplane (above left) was the first real fighter plane. The British BE2c (above right) was used for reconnaissance and observation.

Famous Flyer

Manfred von Richthofen
The Red Baron

Crumbs!

crashzzzz!

Richthofen's nickname was the 'Red Baron' because he was actually a Baron and his Fokker triplane was mainly painted red. Like other fighter pilots, he would fly high above an enemy plane before diving on it. Richthofen was very superstitious and refused to fly without having been kissed by a loved one. He was a hero in Germany and his squadron was known as 'The Flying Circus'. He was shot down and killed on 21 April 1918.

The 1916 French Spad 13

British Bristol BE2c attacked by Manfred von Richthofen in his red Fokker triplane

Twin-gun plane!

The Spad 13 was France's best fighter in World War I. It was the first twin-gun plane as well as being very fast, reaching speeds of 190 km/h.

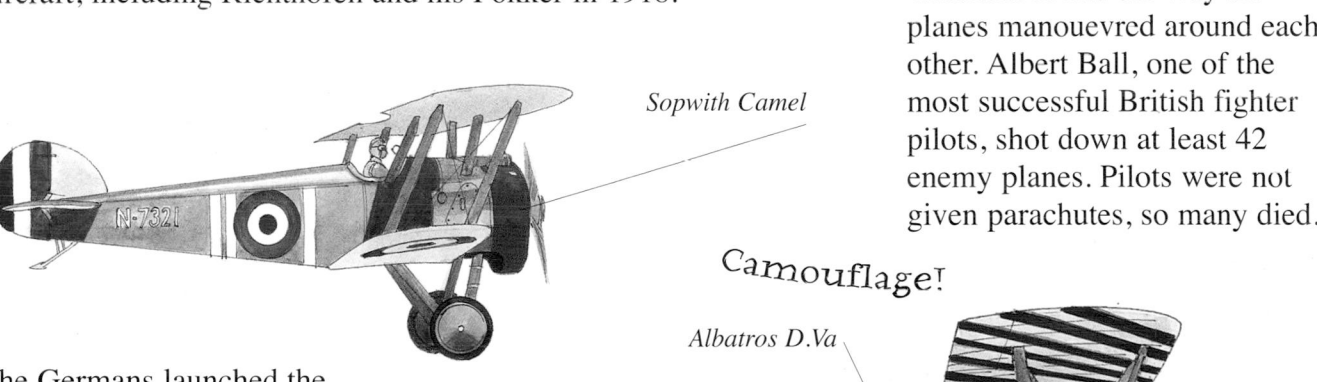

Flying Camels?

The Sopwith Camel was built towards the end of World War I. One of the best British fighters, Camels destroyed over 3,000 enemy aircraft, including Richthofen and his Fokker in 1918.

Sopwith Camel

Dog fights!

Air battles were nicknamed 'dog fights' because of their viciousness and the way the planes manouevred around each other. Albert Ball, one of the most successful British fighter pilots, shot down at least 42 enemy planes. Pilots were not given parachutes, so many died.

Camouflage!

Albatros D.Va

The Germans launched the Albatros D.Va towards the end of World War I. It was a good steady fighter plane, although by then the British were producing planes that were more agile.

The black and white pattern was camouflage that made it hard to see the outline of the plane.

FLYING LONG DISTANCES

In 1919 two British aviators, John Alcock and Arthur Whitten-Brown made the first non-stop flight across the Atlantic. They left Newfoundland, Canada on 14 June, and landed in Ireland 16 hours and 27 minutes later. Only ten years earlier people weren't sure it was possible to fly 37 kilometres across the English Channel! Now men and women all over the world took up the challenge of long-distance flight.

Go Lindy!

Lockheed Sirius

Famous Flyer

Charles Lindbergh

May 1927

American Charles Lindbergh (left) made the first solo trans-Atlantic flight in 1927. Encouraged by a prize of $25,000, he left New York on 20 May, and landed in Paris 33 hours and 30 minutes later. He had flown 5,819 kilometres at an average speed of 173 km/h. In 1931 Lindbergh followed his trans-Atlantic success by pioneering routes across the north Pacific. He and his wife, Anne flew a Lockheed Sirius (above) to Japan via Alaska, Siberia and the Kurile Islands.

First trans-Atlantic flight!

As Lindbergh's plane, the Spirit of St Louis, *approached Paris, the excitement was immense. Overnight he had become the most famous man in the world. The plane was named after his supporters in St Louis, Missouri who helped raise funds for the plane.*

22

Alcock and Brown used a converted Vickers Vimy bomber (left) for their non-stop Atlantic crossing in 1919.

A Curtiss NC4 flying boat (left) made the very first Atlantic crossing. It took 54 hours with several refuelling stops.

In 1926 Richard Byrd flew a Fokker Trimotor (right) to the North Pole.

In 1928 Charles Kingsford Smith used Southern Cross *(right), another Fokker, for the first flight across the Pacific Ocean.*

Amazing Amy!

Women also set long-distance flying records. In 1930, Amy Johnson made the first solo flight from England to Australia. She took 9½ days in her de Havilland Gypsy Moth, taking six days from England to India – a record. In 1932, she made the fastest solo flight from England to South Africa. She died in 1941 after her plane crashed into the River Thames.

Air races!

In July 1933, Wiley Post set out in his plane the Lockheed Vega *Winnie Mae* (left). In this, he made the first solo round-the-world flight covering 24,954 kilometres in 7 days, 19 hours and 49 minutes.

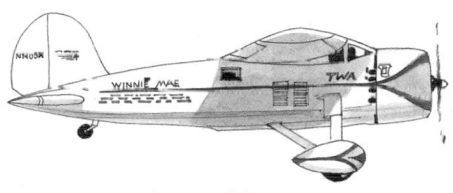

In 1934 the city of Melbourne, Australia, held an air race from England to mark its centenary. The specially built twin-engined DH88 Comet, Grosvenor House *(below) won in 71 hours.*

SHIPS OF THE AIR

Between 1910 and 1914, Zeppelin ran regular passenger services in Germany using airships such as this one

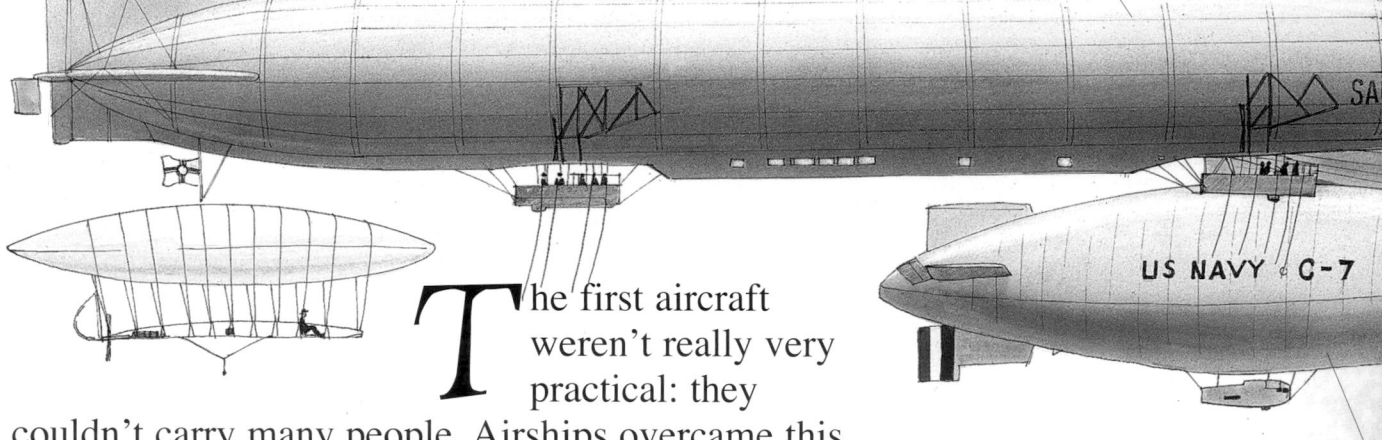

The first aircraft weren't really very practical: they couldn't carry many people. Airships overcame this problem. In 1898 Alberto Santos-Dumont (page 15) built an airship powered by a petrol engine (above). It flew well, but the gas-filled bag keeping it airborne could change shape, making it difficult to control. However, rigid bodies would give airships stability.

US Navy C-7 non-rigid airship

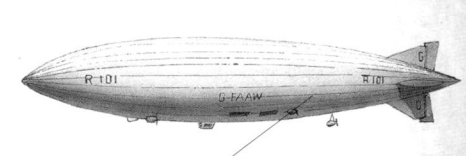

British R101

British interest in airships had ended when its latest ship, the R101, crashed in 1930. Only 8 of the 54 people onboard survived.

Hindenburg Disaster!

Count Ferdinand von Zeppelin began building rigid airships in Germany in 1900. The company's airship service between German cities (top) was extremely popular. In World War I airships were used for reconnaissance and hunting enemy ships. After the war, airlines started airship services between Europe and America, a flight of about three days. In 1937 the Hindenburg caught fire while docking in New Jersey, killing 35 of the 97 people on board. The era of airships ended that day.

CRAAASSSSH!

KABOOOM!

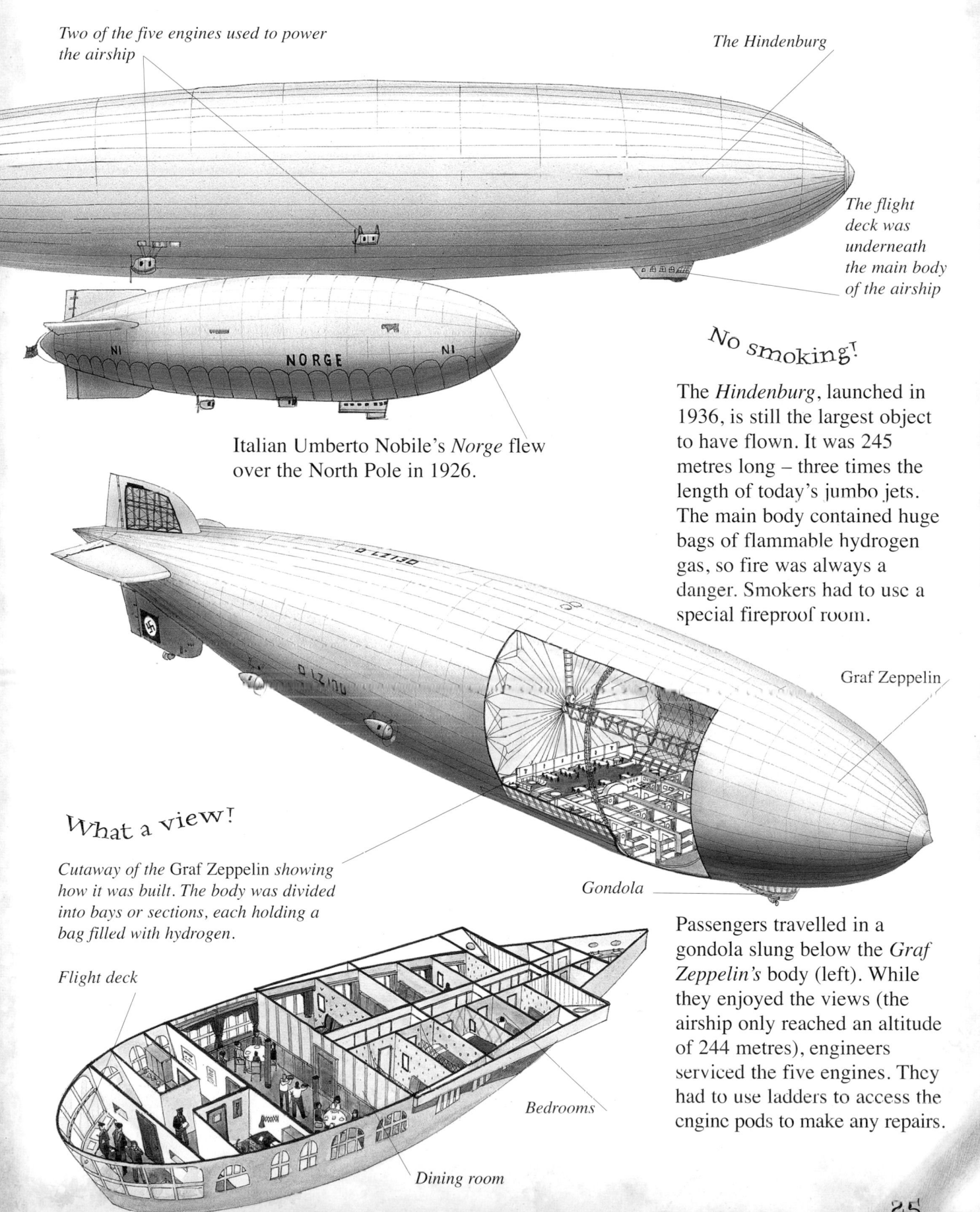

Two of the five engines used to power the airship

The Hindenburg

The flight deck was underneath the main body of the airship

Italian Umberto Nobile's *Norge* flew over the North Pole in 1926.

No smoking!

The *Hindenburg*, launched in 1936, is still the largest object to have flown. It was 245 metres long – three times the length of today's jumbo jets. The main body contained huge bags of flammable hydrogen gas, so fire was always a danger. Smokers had to use a special fireproof room.

Graf Zeppelin

What a view!

Cutaway of the Graf Zeppelin *showing how it was built. The body was divided into bays or sections, each holding a bag filled with hydrogen.*

Gondola

Flight deck

Bedrooms

Dining room

Passengers travelled in a gondola slung below the *Graf Zeppelin's* body (left). While they enjoyed the views (the airship only reached an altitude of 244 metres), engineers serviced the five engines. They had to use ladders to access the engine pods to make any repairs.

25

TRAVEL BY AIR AND SEA

It was soon obvious that planes offered a practical way of travelling long distances. But they needed somewhere to land. Water was the obvious answer because although there were no airports then, there were plenty of ports and harbours. Frenchman Henri Fabre fitted floats, not wheels, to his plane and successfully took off from water in 1910 – the first person to do so. From this developed the 'flying boats', as the aircraft were called, that successfully carried passengers and cargo throughout the 1920s and 1930s.

Air mail!

In the 1930s Britain's Imperial Airways (the forerunner of today's British Airways), had a fleet of Empire class flying boats for its long-distance routes. As well as carrying up to 24 passengers, the flying boats carried mail. During World War II flying boats were used as patrol and rescue planes, helping to save many lives. However once the war ended, flying boats were phased out and replaced by the first modern airliners, which were much cheaper to build.

Famous Flyers

Flying Boats!

Tail

Aft cabin

Midship cabin

Baggage and mail hold

Rear propeller

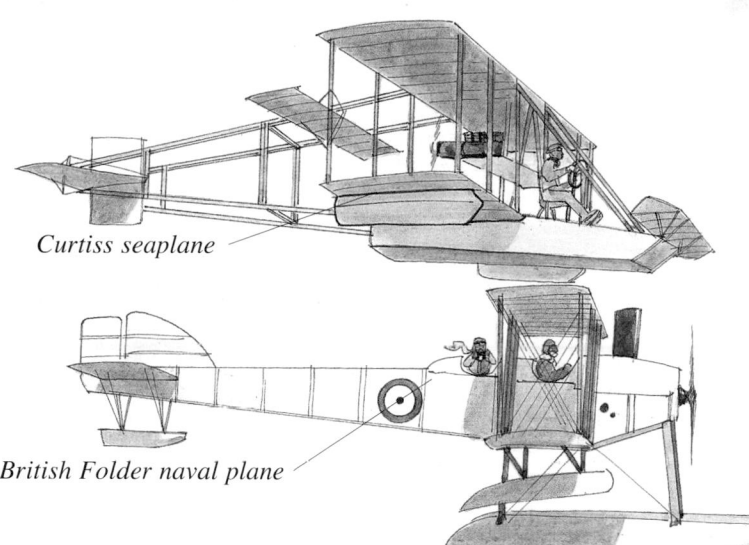

Curtiss seaplane

Hydravion, *Henri Fabre's seaplane,* had its propeller at the back

British Folder naval plane

In 1913 a Curtiss seaplane climbed to 1,890 metres setting a new altitude record.

Folding planes!

The Folder (above) was used for reconnaissance in World War I. When needed, its wings were unfolded and it was lowered onto the sea.

Italian Caproni Ca-60

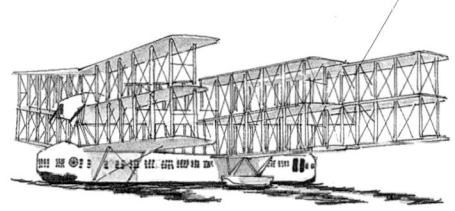

The Italian Caproni CA-60 triplane (left) had eight engines and was designed to carry 100 passengers across the Atlantic. It crashed on its maiden flight in March 1921.

Engine inspection hatch

Bristol Pegasus engines

Direction finding aerial

Flight deck

Mooring hatch

RCE

In 1930, Costes and Bellonte made the first east-west crossing of the north Atlantic from Europe to the USA. They used a Dornier-Wal flying boat (below).

Crossing the Atlantic!

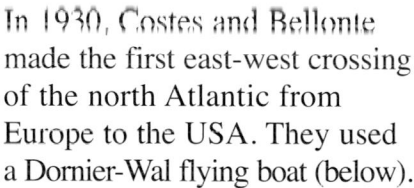

German Dornier-Wal

The Dornier Do X (right) could carry 170 passengers. It flew from Europe, via Africa and South America to New York. But it was ahead of its time and the 12 engines it used were not powerful enough for it.

27

ACROSS THE WORLD

Gradually designers and engineers came to understand more and more about the science of flying. As a result, aircraft become safer and more reliable. Once the general public became aware of this, they too wanted to fly. Soon flying became fashionable, at least among those who could afford it. Imagine a world without airports, security checks or traffic-clogged journeys to or from the airport! That is what air travel was like at first.

Pan American Airways built a reputation for long-distance flights (logo far left), especially across the Pacific and Atlantic Oceans.

Famous Flights

Long Distance Air Travel

That's a big flying fish!

Sky high prices!

Flights from the US to Hong Kong took five or six days. The planes had to stop to refuel and navigating at night was difficult and dangerous. Planes left San Francisco then flew via Hawaii over the Pacific to Hong Kong. As tickets were so expensive, only the very rich could afford to fly, and it would be several years before planes overtook trains as the favourite way to travel long distances.

Piggyback planes!

In 1938 these two aircraft (left) set a record for a straight-line seaplane flight. The larger *Maia* lifted the much smaller *Mercury* into the air so it wasted no fuel in take off. Mercury then went on to make a record east-west crossing which was also the first commercial flight over the North Atlantic.

The triple-fin tail unit gave greater stability

The Boeing 314 Clipper *had four Wright Twin Cyclone engines*

The Clipper's anchor was housed in the nose

How big was it?

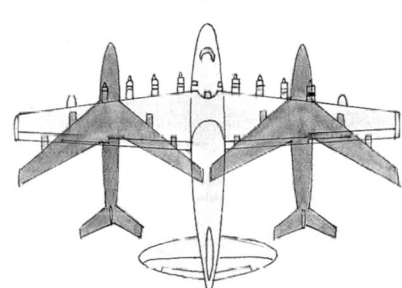

Spruce Goose, *the giant flying boat built by Howard Hughes, is shown above with two Boeing 707s for comparison.*

Clear skies - essential!

The big Boeing 314 *Clipper* flying boat (above) could take 74 passengers because it had to carry so much fuel. In the 1930s planes did not have night navigation aids. If the *Clipper* flew at night the crew navigated by the stars – just as if they were on a ship!

Spruce Goose

Giant wooden plane!

Howard Hughes's H4 Hercules, *Spruce Goose* (right), was wooden and would have gone into production if the US had run short of metals in World War II. Fortunately there was no shortage. Hughes made a short flight in it in 1947.

AIRLINES AND AIRLINERS

After the First World War, countries found they had lots of planes and pilots with nothing to do. In the USA old bombers were used to carry mail long distances. It was dangerous work and 30 of the first 40 mail pilots were killed in accidents. In February 1919, a daily service between Berlin and Weimar began in Germany – taking two passengers on each flight! In August, the first international service, between London and Paris, started – and so did the age of air travel.

Splash landings!

The Sikorsky S-38 of 1928 (above) could land on airstrips or water. Pan American used it for its Caribbean services.

Famous Flyer
Ellen Church
First airline stewardess

In 1930, United Airlines became the first airline to employ female air stewardesses. Ellen Church, a trained nurse from Iowa in the USA was one. Previously, only men had done the job, and some airlines resisted using female stewardesses for many years.

Welcome aboard, please take your seat.

SCYL

30

Douglas DC-2: USA

Savoia Marchetti SM74: Italy

Junkers Ju 52: Germany

Wibault-penhoet 282-T-12: France

From dropping bombs to carrying passengers!

The world's first airliners were based on World War I bombers. Gradually airlines introduced planes designed for people (above). But in World War II the German Junkers Ju 52 was adapted for military use.

The best airliners of the 1930s were the Douglas DC-2 (top) and the later DC-3. These aircraft were streamlined and economical. Britain's Imperial Airways, however, continued to use many older designs, including the Short *Scylla* (below), based on biplanes.

Jack Sanderson, one of the first airline stewards, worked for Britain's Daimler Airways. He died in a crash between London and Paris in 1923.

How embarrassing!?

Imperial Airways' four-engined Short *Scylla* carried 39 passengers in three cabins, but was difficult to fly in bad weather. The airline also used the Handley Page HP42. In the 1930s this biplane airliner carried more passengers between London and Europe than all other airlines combined.

Weight was an important consideration and passengers were weighed with their luggage.

IMPROVING ALL THE TIME

Twenty years after the Wrights proved flying was possible, aircraft were becoming an important part of everyday life. Companies started making them, airlines used them (left, logo of German airline Lufthansa) and the rich flew in them. The basics of flight were understood and aircraft were becoming safer as designers and engineers introduced improvements. But the problems of helicopter flight remained unsolved. After a break of 30 years Igor Sikorsky (page 15) returned to his research – and found the answer.

Luxury . . . for some!

While the passengers sat in comfort in the Imperial Airways' 'Silver Wing' Argosy (the world's first named flight), the pilots had to put up with an open cockpit. The route was between London and Paris in 1927.

Famous Flight

First flight of

VS-300 helicopter

Whirrrrrr

14 September

1939

Whirrrrrr

Success at last!

Igor Sikorsky added a small rear rotor to his VS-300. This prevented the helicopter spinning or twisting as it flew. Now there was another useful flying machine. Sikorsky continued to make improvements to the VS-300, and by summer 1940 it could stay in the air for 15 minutes at a time.

The German Junkers F13 – the first modern commercial aircraft

The Junkers F13 was the first all-metal aircraft built to carry both cargo and passengers.

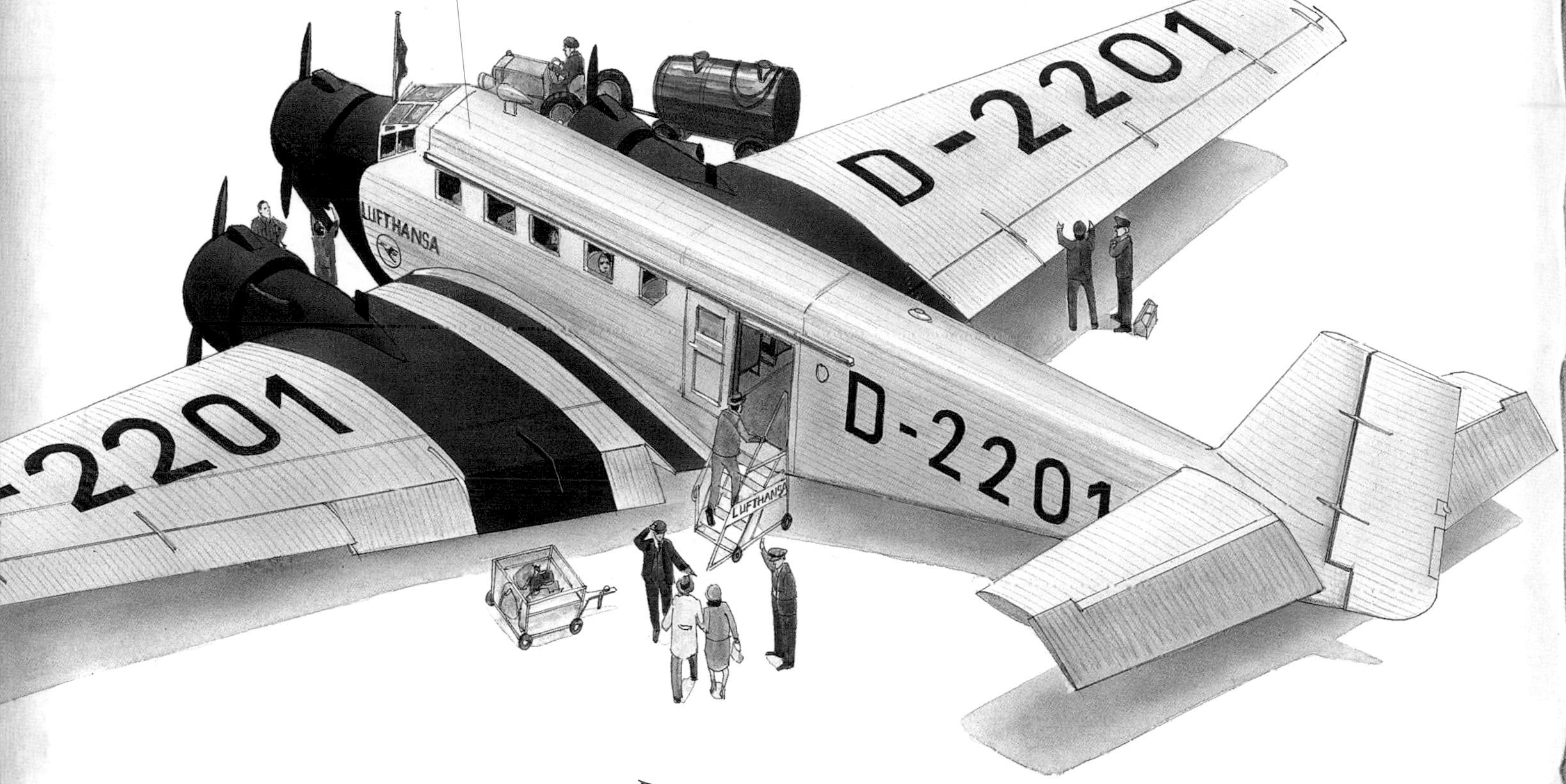

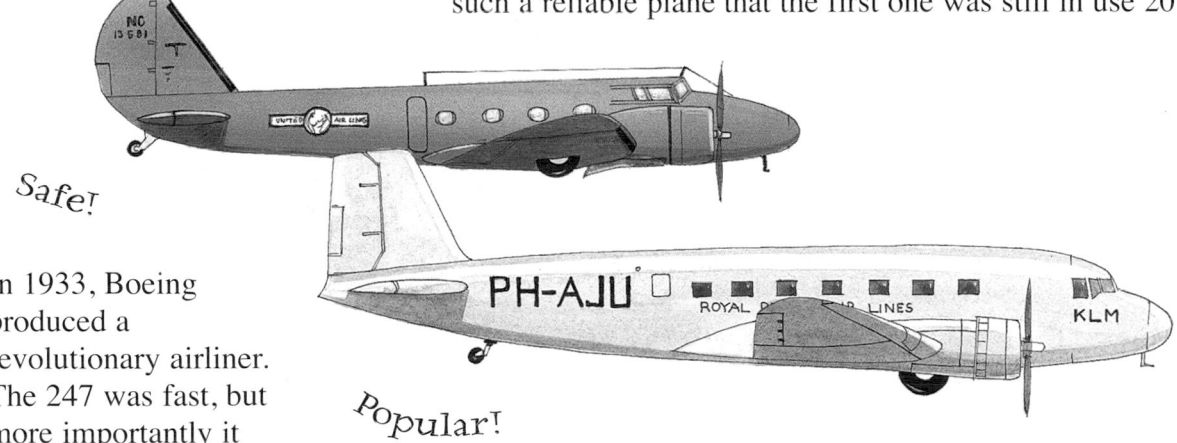

Reliable!

The F13 started flying passengers and cargo in 1919 before Lufthansa, the German national airline, was founded in 1926. It was such a reliable plane that the first one was still in use 20 years later.

Safe!

In 1933, Boeing produced a revolutionary airliner. The 247 was fast, but more importantly it could still fly if one of its engines failed.

Popular!

In 1935, the most popular airliner ever started flying. The Douglas DC-3, or *Dakota*, was the successor of the DC-2. Like the earlier plane, the DC-3 was streamlined and had retractable landing gear. Well-built and reliable, many DC-3s are still in use although the last one was built in 1948.

33

BLITZKRIEG!

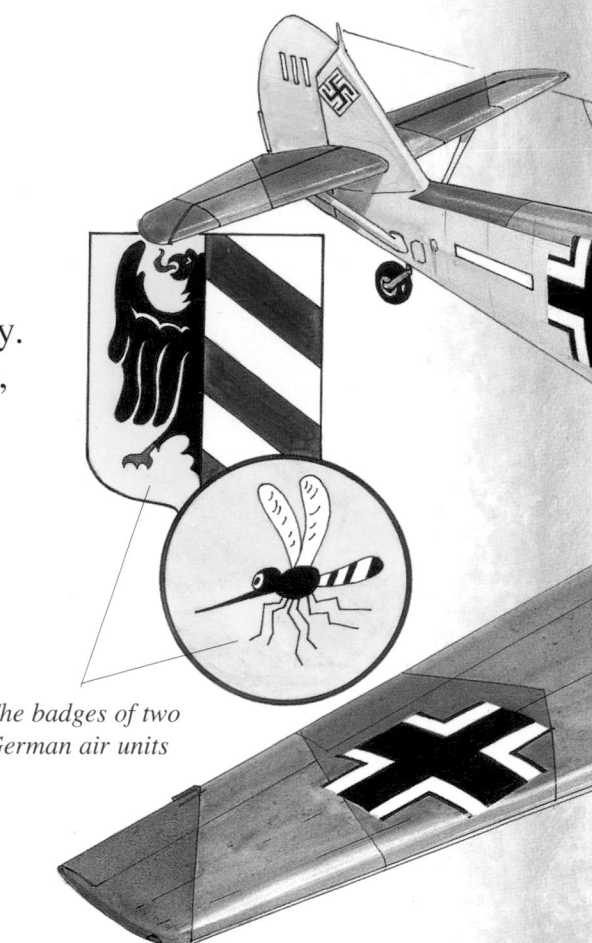

Throughout the 1930s, the political picture in Europe grew increasingly bleak. In 1933, Adolf Hitler was elected Chancellor of Germany. He lead the right-wing National Socialist (Nazi) party, established a dictatorship, and started rearming Germany, breaking the peace agreement after World War I. An admirer of the British Empire, Hitler also wanted overseas possessions and began an aggressive foreign policy of invasion called *Blitzkrieg* or 'lightning war'. Aircraft like the Stuka (top left) were vital to his plans.

The badges of two German air units

Famous Aviation Moment
Blitzkrieg!
1940

Spoilsport.

Get down!

Boing!
Boing!
Boing!

The Messerschmitt Bf 109 was the best fighter plane the *Luftwaffe* (German air force) had. Over 30,000 were built between 1939 and 1945.

Flying pencils?

The Dornier Do-17 (below) was nicknamed the 'Flying Pencil' because of its very long thin fuselage.

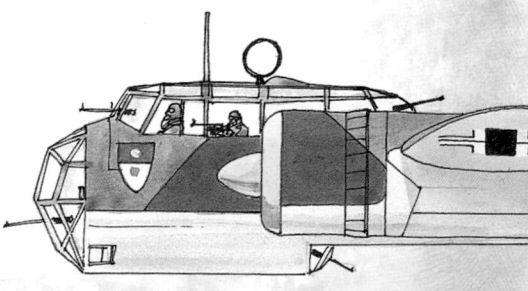

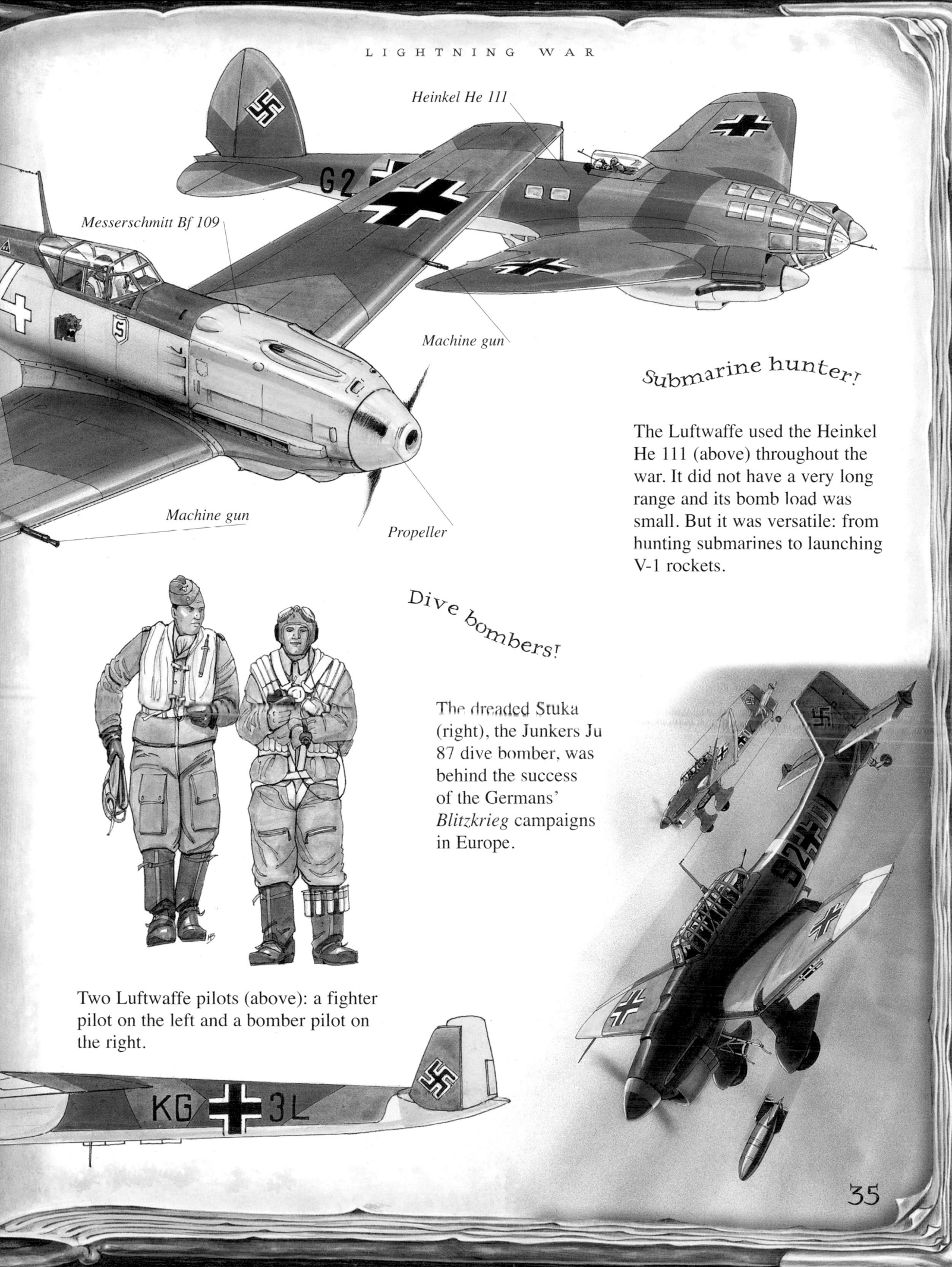

Heinkel He 111

Messerschmitt Bf 109

Machine gun

Machine gun

Propeller

Submarine hunter!

The Luftwaffe used the Heinkel He 111 (above) throughout the war. It did not have a very long range and its bomb load was small. But it was versatile: from hunting submarines to launching V-1 rockets.

Dive bombers!

The dreaded Stuka (right), the Junkers Ju 87 dive bomber, was behind the success of the Germans' *Blitzkrieg* campaigns in Europe.

Two Luftwaffe pilots (above): a fighter pilot on the left and a bomber pilot on the right.

THE BATTLE OF BRITAIN

hen war was declared in 1939 only the Royal Air Force (RAF) opposed the Luftwaffe. Germany had invaded France, Belgium and the Netherlands and the USA did not enter the war until 1941. Italy was allied with Germany, and Spain was neutral. Hitler had been building up the Luftwaffe for years while British politicians tried to make treaties with him. It soon became clear that initially at least, Britain's safety depended on the success of its air defences.

The RAF's 'Wings' badge (below). The RAF was formed in 1918 from the Royal Flying Corps founded in 1912 and Royal Naval Air Service founded in 1914.

Famous Aviation Moment
The Battle of Britain
1940

This was their finest hour.

Winston Churchill

Outnumbered!

The aerial fighting in summer 1940 became known as 'the Battle of Britain'. Three thousand Luftwaffe planes were pitched against the RAF who had less than a thousand. The heart of the British defences were Spitfires (top right) and Hurricanes (bottom right). Both sides lost many men and planes. The heavy losses suffered by Britain would have been much worse without the efforts of the RAF. Gradually the battle turned against the Luftwaffe as British planes were fitted with a new radar warning system. This warned of German attacks, so the Spitfires and Hurricanes could be ready in position to attack the enemy planes.

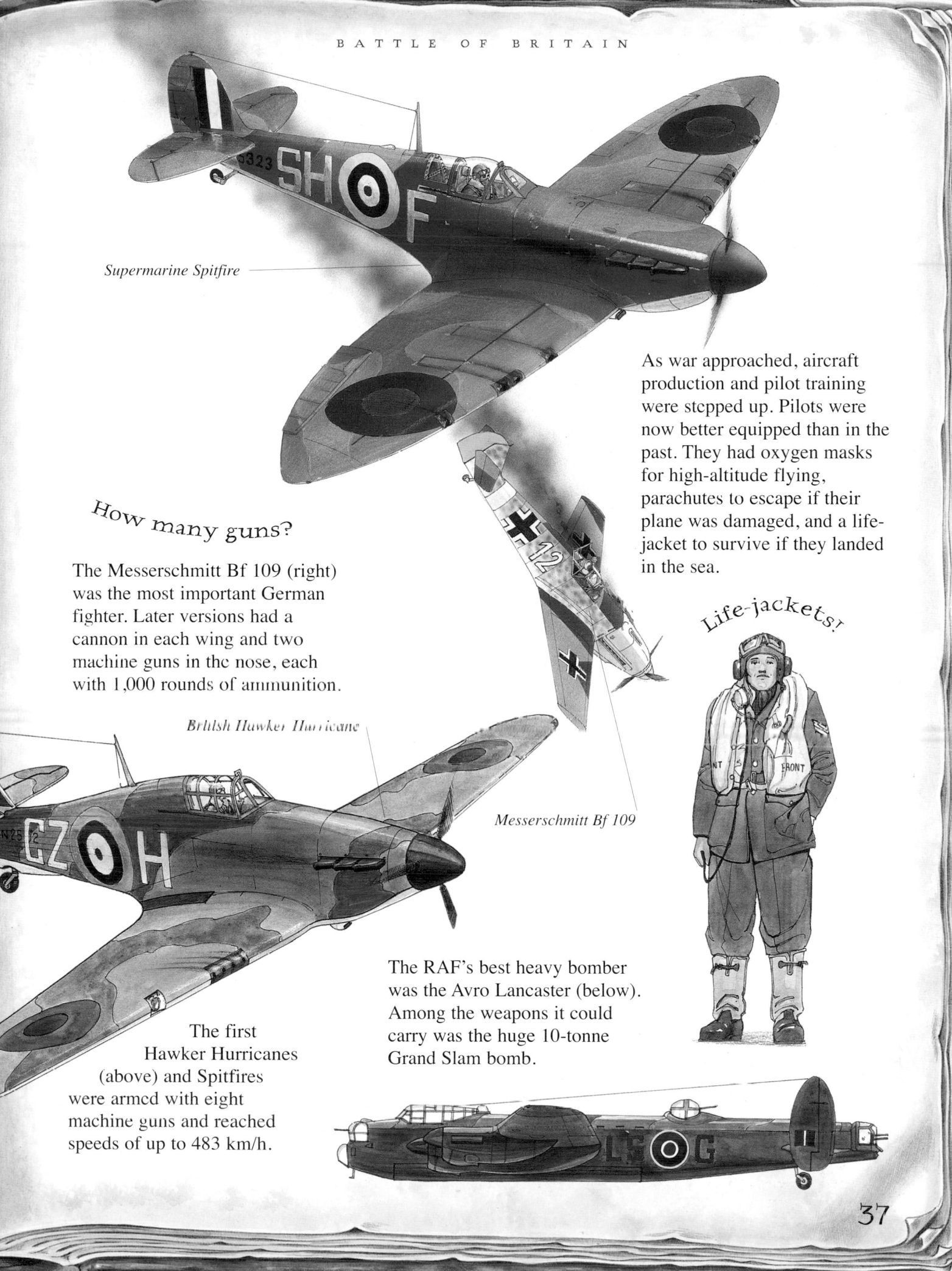

Supermarine Spitfire

As war approached, aircraft production and pilot training were stepped up. Pilots were now better equipped than in the past. They had oxygen masks for high-altitude flying, parachutes to escape if their plane was damaged, and a life-jacket to survive if they landed in the sea.

How many guns?

The Messerschmitt Bf 109 (right) was the most important German fighter. Later versions had a cannon in each wing and two machine guns in the nose, each with 1,000 rounds of ammunition.

British Hawker Hurricane

Messerschmitt Bf 109

Life-jackets!

The RAF's best heavy bomber was the Avro Lancaster (below). Among the weapons it could carry was the huge 10-tonne Grand Slam bomb.

The first Hawker Hurricanes (above) and Spitfires were armed with eight machine guns and reached speeds of up to 483 km/h.

AMERICA UNDER ATTACK

B y October 1940, the Battle of Britain was over, although the Luftwaffe continued night raids on British cities. Hitler decided not to invade Britain, and the focus of the war shifted east to the Pacific. Despite the efforts of Winston Churchill, the British prime minister, the Americans still refused to enter the war. Then, on 7 December 1941, the Japanese attacked the US fleet at Pearl Harbour, Hawaii. Enraged, America at last joined Britain, France and the other allies in the war.

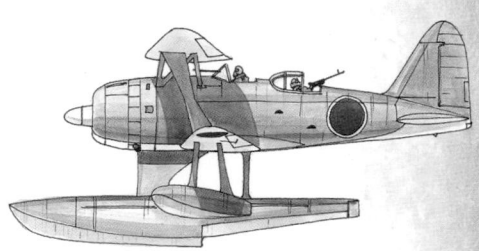

Mitsubishi F1M2 sea biplane used for short-range reconnaissance (above).

Kamikaze (Japanese for 'divine wind') pilots crashed their planes into a target.

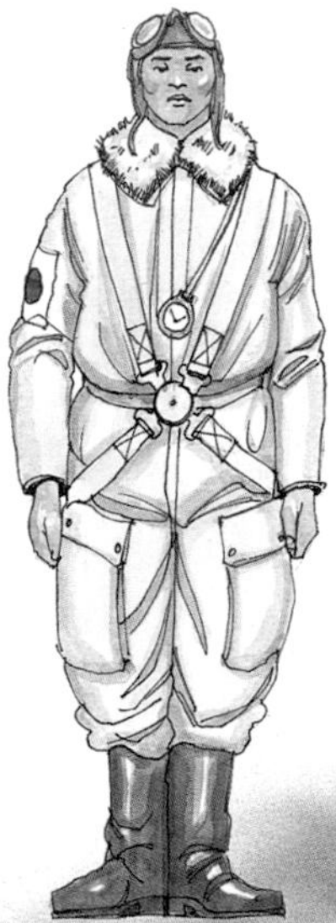

Famous Flyers

Japanese Kamikaze Pilots

1943

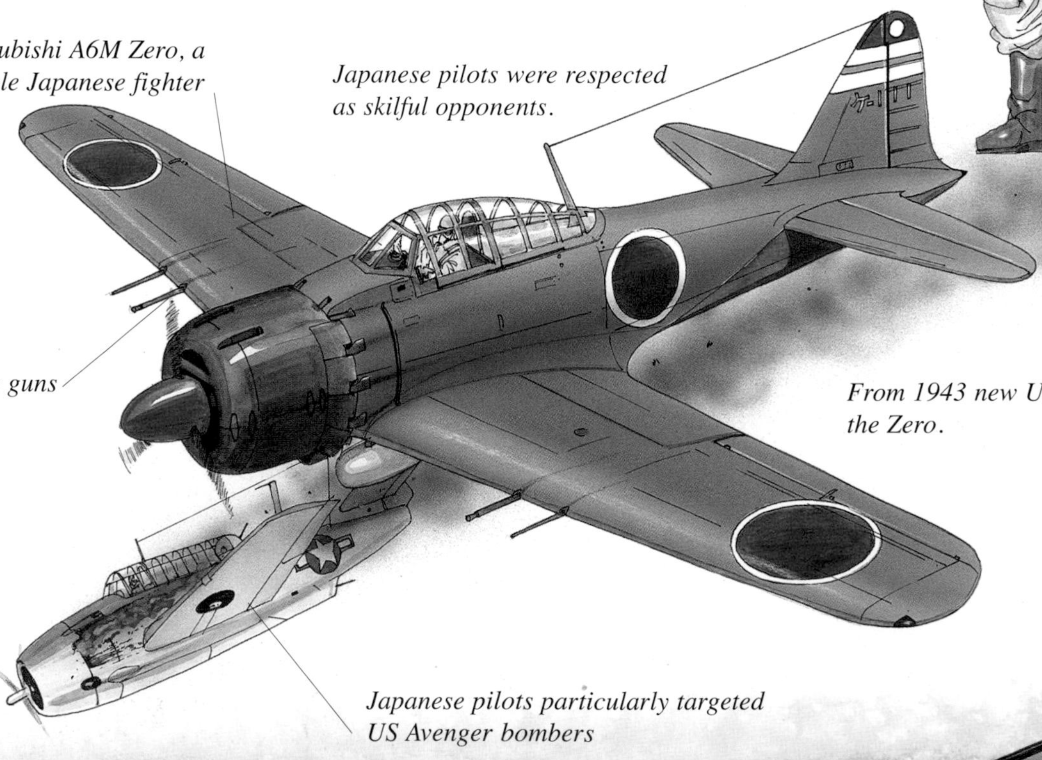

The Mitsubishi A6M Zero, a formidable Japanese fighter

Japanese pilots were respected as skilful opponents.

Machine guns

From 1943 new US fighters outclassed the Zero.

Japanese pilots particularly targeted US Avenger bombers

Dive bombers!

The Aichi D3A dive bomber (left) spearheaded Japan's attack on Pearl Harbour in 1941. They also used it in 1942 in the Battle of Midway which Japan went on to lose.

Badges!

"MEMPHIS BELLE"

Many pilots put badges on their B-17s. Memphis Belle (above) was the most famous.

At least we can see what we're shooting at in the daytime!

There were many US airbases in Britain because planes then could not fly the long distances they can today. Pilots of the US Air Force (left) carried out daytime raids, while the RAF bombed at night.

Flight deck

Machine guns

Machine guns

Bomb doors open during a raid

The powerful Boeing B-17 (Flying Fortress) bomber.

39

INTO THE JET AGE

How do they work?

Aircraft design continued improving as each country tried to have the best planes. Speed was important and this meant better engines. On a test flight in May 1941, a plane powered by Frank Whittle's jet engine reached 560 km/h. The engineer Hans Joachim Pabst von Ohain was doing similar work in Germany at this time and designed the first operational jet engine. His jet engine powered a Heinkel He 178 in August 1939, but this experimental plane never flew again.

Jet engines work by sucking air in at the front, compressing and burning it to produce gas which gives a forward thrust as it escapes at the rear of the engine. At first Whittle had problems with his engine because it was too advanced for the technology of the time. The materials had to be immensely strong to withstand the engine's high speeds and temperatures.

Famous Aviation Moment
Frank Whittle patents the jet engine 1930

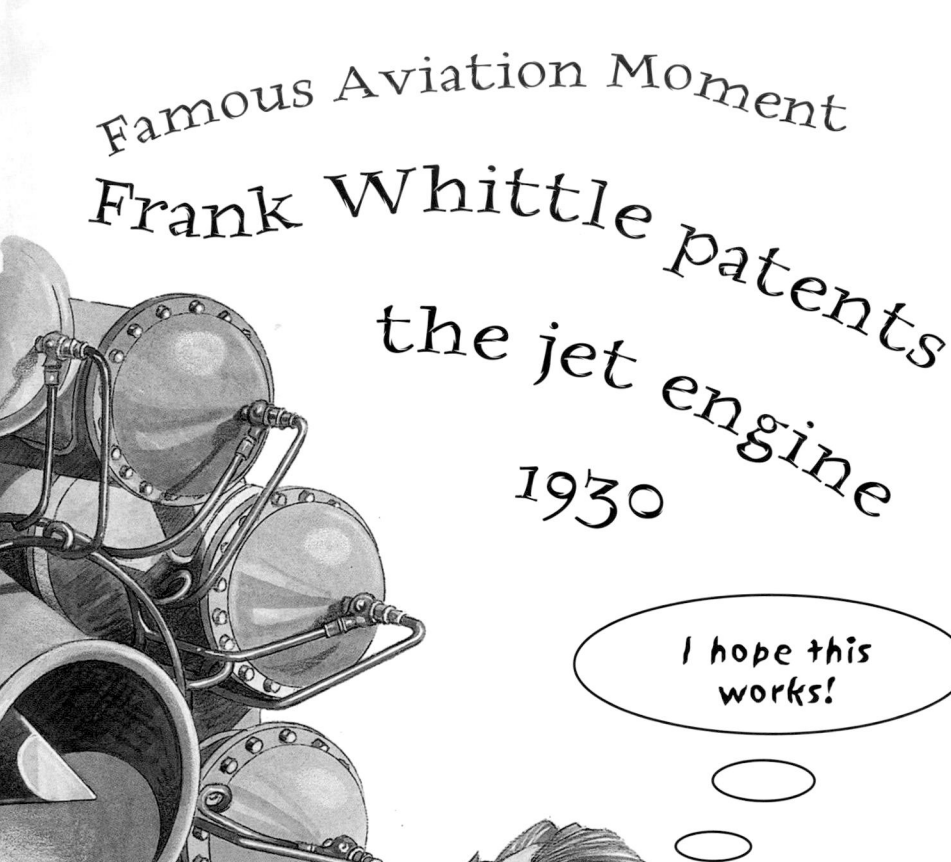

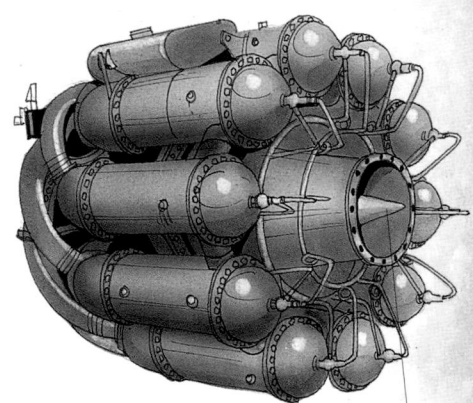

Rear view of Whittle's engine showing the exhaust

I hope this works!

In Whittle's early engines, the combustion chambers (where the air was turned into gas), often cracked and sometimes exploded! Even when these problems were overcome, the RAF took a lot of persuading that this was the aircraft engine of the future. After the war, he retired from the RAF with the rank of Air Commodore and Queen Elizabeth II honoured his achievements with a knighthood in 1976.

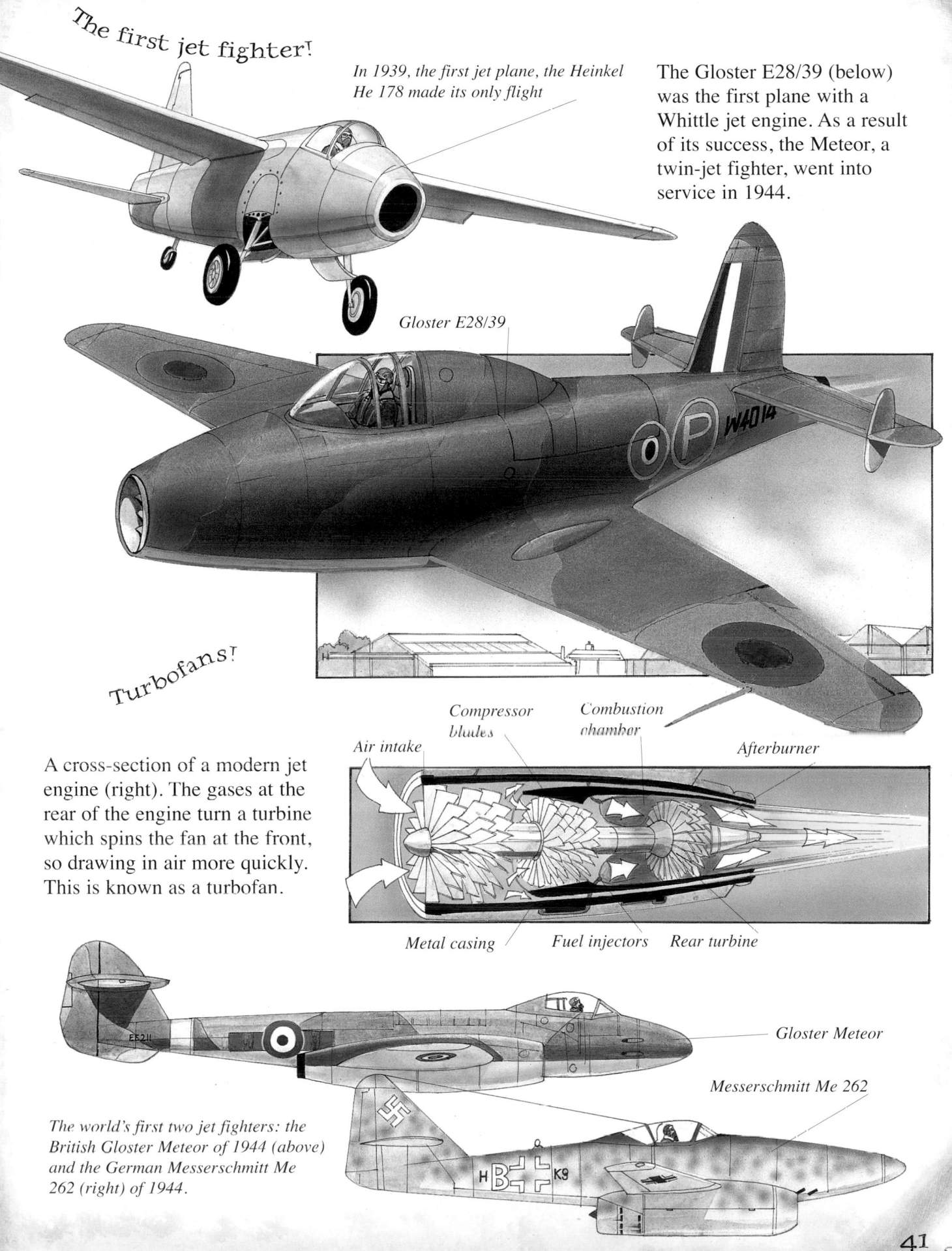

The first jet fighter!

In 1939, the first jet plane, the Heinkel He 178 made its only flight

The Gloster E28/39 (below) was the first plane with a Whittle jet engine. As a result of its success, the Meteor, a twin-jet fighter, went into service in 1944.

Gloster E28/39

W4014

Turbofans!

A cross-section of a modern jet engine (right). The gases at the rear of the engine turn a turbine which spins the fan at the front, so drawing in air more quickly. This is known as a turbofan.

Compressor blades

Combustion chamber

Air intake

Afterburner

Metal casing　*Fuel injectors*　*Rear turbine*

EE211

Gloster Meteor

Messerschmitt Me 262

The world's first two jet fighters: the British Gloster Meteor of 1944 (above) and the German Messerschmitt Me 262 (right) of 1944.

41

A NEW WAR BEGINS

Almost as soon as World War II ended another war began. Historians call it the 'Cold War'. Although there were conventional wars, such as the Korean War (1950-53) and the Vietnam War (1964-75), the Cold War was psychological rather than military, with each side spying and putting political pressure on the other. And who were the enemies? It was really two political systems: communism and democracy, with the USSR (part of modern day Russia) and the US leading the two sides.

Spy planes!

Spying was a crucial part of the Cold War. The best planes for this flew at very high altitudes and were designed to evade radar and other means of detection.

Famous Aviation Moments

Korean and Vietnam Wars

Sabre F-86 used by the US in the Korean War

The era of jet engines meant higher speeds and more agile planes. As a result, aerial combat was faster and more vicious than ever.

Russian built MiG-15s flown by the Communist forces

One of the worst conflicts of the Cold War was the Vietnam War. In 1964, US forces invaded Vietnam to support the non-communist South against the communist North. In 1973, after suffering heavy losses, the Americans withdrew. The war finally ended in 1975. Faced by determined resistance and a guerrilla war, US forces needed swift, manoeuvrable transport – the helicopter was ideal. An unarmed Chinook CH-47 (above) carried around 40 fully equipped soldiers. It could hover just above the swamps in which much of the fighting took place. It was also useful for rescuing besieged troops.

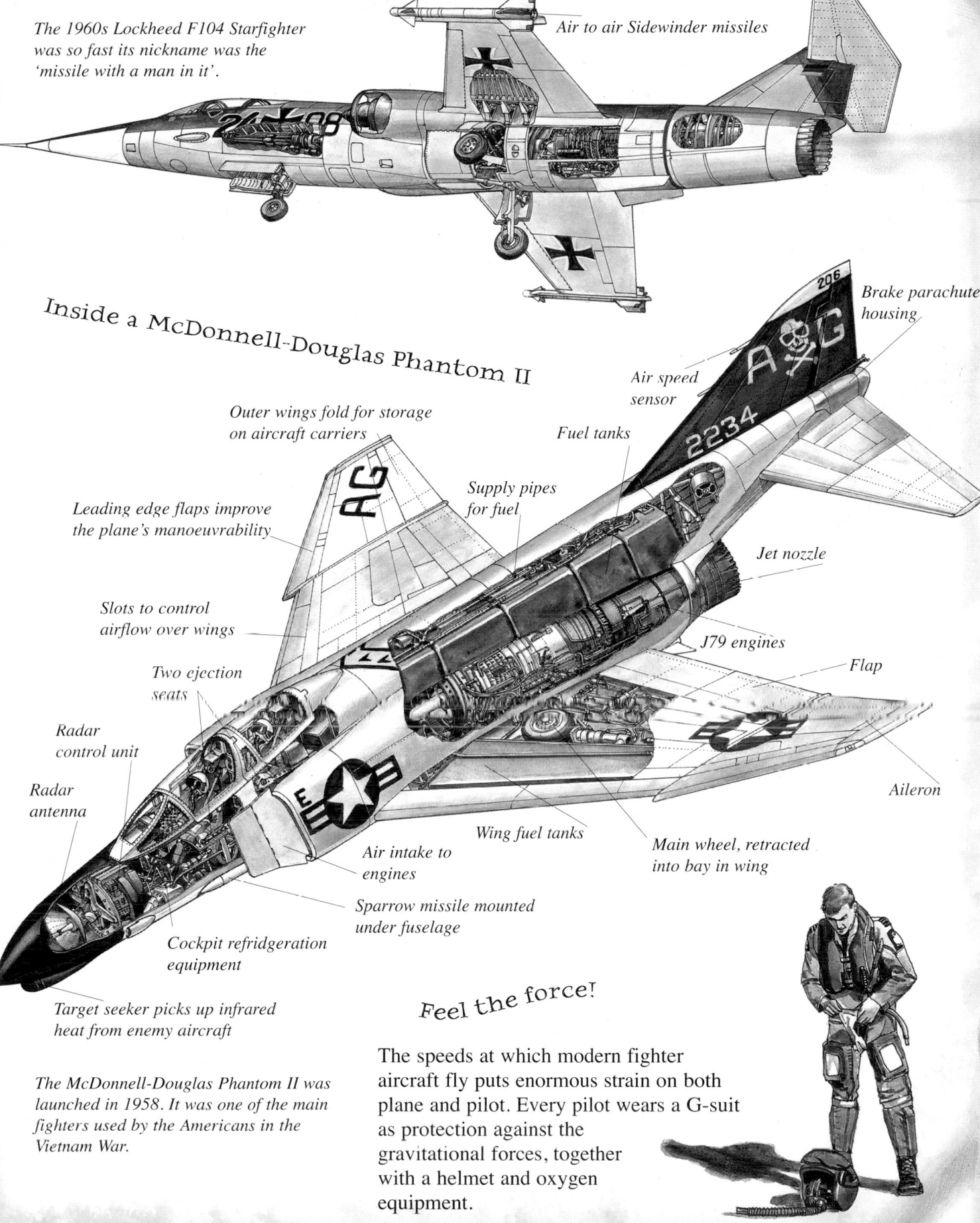

The 1960s Lockheed F104 Starfighter was so fast its nickname was the 'missile with a man in it'.

Air to air Sidewinder missiles

Inside a McDonnell-Douglas Phantom II

Outer wings fold for storage on aircraft carriers

Leading edge flaps improve the plane's manoeuvrability

Slots to control airflow over wings

Two ejection seats

Radar control unit

Radar antenna

Cockpit refridgeration equipment

Target seeker picks up infrared heat from enemy aircraft

Air intake to engines

Sparrow missile mounted under fuselage

Supply pipes for fuel

Fuel tanks

Air speed sensor

Brake parachute housing

Jet nozzle

J79 engines

Flap

Aileron

Main wheel, retracted into bay in wing

Wing fuel tanks

The McDonnell-Douglas Phantom II was launched in 1958. It was one of the main fighters used by the Americans in the Vietnam War.

Feel the force!

The speeds at which modern fighter aircraft fly puts enormous strain on both plane and pilot. Every pilot wears a G-suit as protection against the gravitational forces, together with a helmet and oxygen equipment.

43

THE FASTEST FLYERS

As soon as flight was possible, everyone wanted to go faster and higher. Just sixty years after Orville Wright flew three metres above ground the American built rocket-powered X-15 reached an altitude of 107 kilometres! (Mount Everest, the world's highest mountain, is 8.8 kilometres high). Many pilots were killed in this quest for speed, but research into why accidents happened led to greater safety.

Breaking the sound barrier!

In 1947, American pilot Chuck Yeager broke the sound barrier – flying faster than the speed of sound (1224 km/h) – in a Bell X-1 rocket plane.

Too hot to handle!

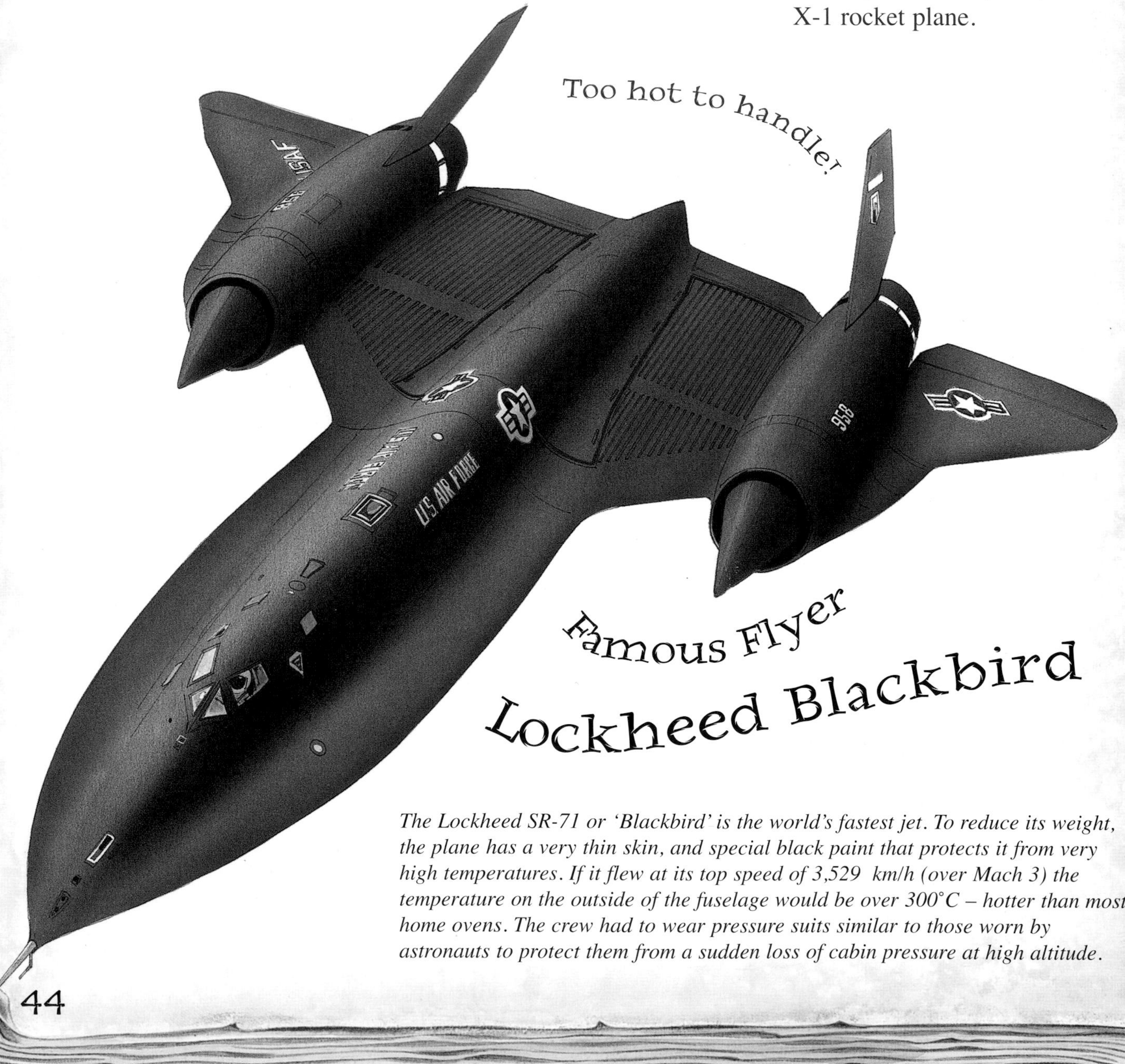

Famous Flyer
Lockheed Blackbird

The Lockheed SR-71 or 'Blackbird' is the world's fastest jet. To reduce its weight, the plane has a very thin skin, and special black paint that protects it from very high temperatures. If it flew at its top speed of 3,529 km/h (over Mach 3) the temperature on the outside of the fuselage would be over 300°C – hotter than most home ovens. The crew had to wear pressure suits similar to those worn by astronauts to protect them from a sudden loss of cabin pressure at high altitude.

The X-15 is the fastest manned winged aircraft in the world. On 3 October 1967, it flew at Mach 6.7 – over six times the speed of sound. To date, this record has not been beaten.

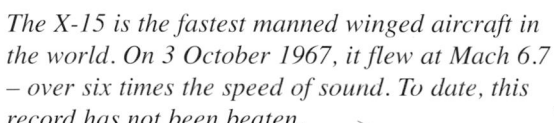

Still unbeaten for speed!

The X-15 was launched from below a B-52 bomber that carried it to a high altitude to save fuel. It also set an altitude records later that same month when pilot William 'Pete' Knight flew to over 85 kilometres. The X-15 made a huge impact on the development of the US space programme.

Scramjets!

X-43A

If you don't need to worry about the effects of G-force on a pilot, you can fly even faster. NASA's X-43A holds the record for the fastest unmanned flight at Mach 9.6 - that's 11,265 km/h! This is possible thanks to new technology. Supersonic combustion ramjets (scramjets) work differently to conventional jet engines and have no rotating parts.

The best of the rest!

The US Air Force's B-2 Stealth bomber (above left) has a 'flying wing' design meaning the plane is essentially one giant wing, like a boomerang. This shape combined with the radar-absorbent surface makes it very difficult to detect.

Another successful combat aircraft is the Boeing F15-E Eagle (left), launched by the US Air Force in 1988. It can fly at altitudes of 18,000 metres and speeds of Mach 2.5 (over twice the speed of sound).

45

HELICOPTERS

Was this machine (left) sketched by Leonardo da Vinci around 1500, the inspiration for helicopters? If it was, he was about 500 years ahead of his time. In 1907 the helicopter made by the French pioneer Paul Cornu got 30 centimetres off the ground. But Cornu ran out of money and made no more helicopters. The first successful helicopter, the German Focke-Wulf Fw 61 did not fly until 1936.

The top-mounted rotor blades on a helicopter create the lift to make it airborne.

The Sikorsky R-4 Hoverfly was used by the Allied forces in World War II.

Famous Flyer
James Bond's Autogyro

Whirrrr   Whirrrr

I hope I don't get shaken OR stirred.

Sikorsky R-4 Hoverfly

The Wallis autogyro appeared in the James Bond film You Only Live Twice. *It has both an engine and a propeller to make the unpowered rotor blades spin fast enough for lift off.*

Rear pusher-propeller

ARMY

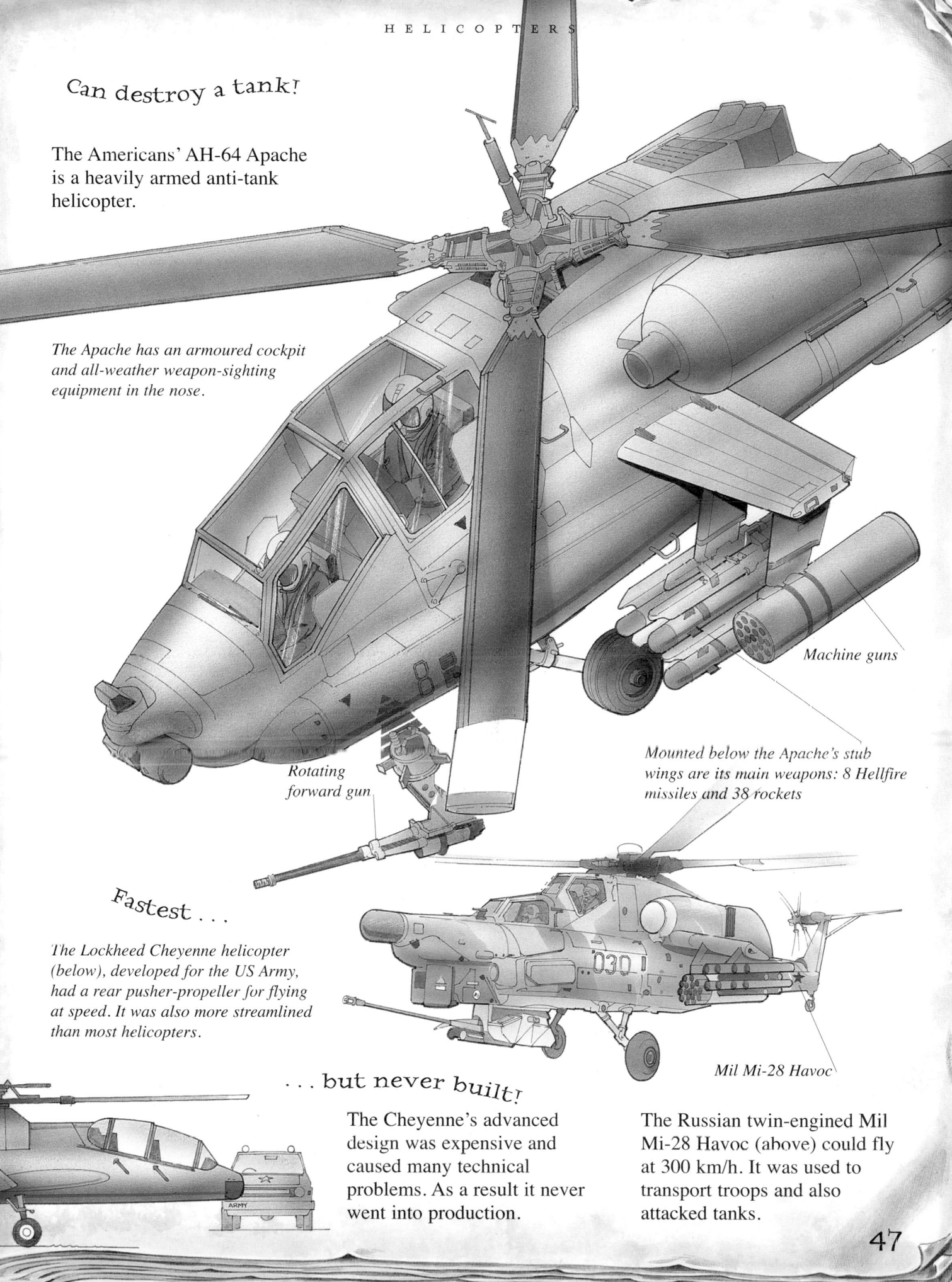

Can destroy a tank!

The Americans' AH-64 Apache is a heavily armed anti-tank helicopter.

The Apache has an armoured cockpit and all-weather weapon-sighting equipment in the nose.

Machine guns

Rotating forward gun

Mounted below the Apache's stub wings are its main weapons: 8 Hellfire missiles and 38 rockets

Fastest . . .

The Lockheed Cheyenne helicopter (below), developed for the US Army, had a rear pusher-propeller for flying at speed. It was also more streamlined than most helicopters.

Mil Mi-28 Havoc

. . . but never built!

The Cheyenne's advanced design was expensive and caused many technical problems. As a result it never went into production.

The Russian twin-engined Mil Mi-28 Havoc (above) could fly at 300 km/h. It was used to transport troops and also attacked tanks.

AIRPORTS AND AIRLINES

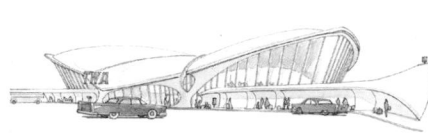

In the 1920s and 1930s airports like today's didn't exist. Aircraft were light enough to take off and land on grass. So that's what airports were: a grassy field with a small terminal building. From these came today's airports. As planes got bigger they became heavier. To stop them sinking into the ground, concrete runways were introduced. Bigger planes meant more passengers. Eventually airport operators realised they could even make money from passengers on the ground!

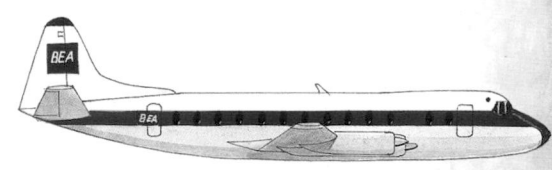

The Vickers Viscount was the most successful British airliner of the late 1940s and 1950s. Its turboprop engines were a combination of propellers and jet engines.

Famous Flyers
Everybody!

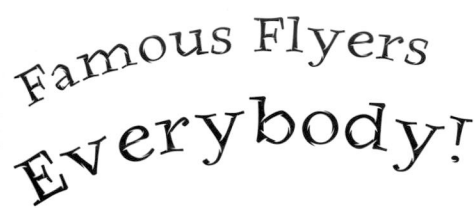

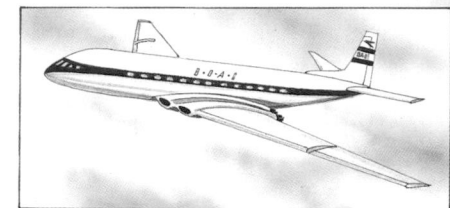

The de Havilland Comet, the first commercial jet airliner, began service in 1952. It had a cruising speed of 784 km/h, but was grounded in 1954 after serious accidents.

We're cleared to land, Roger.

'Roger' is a term used by aviation workers and means 'Message received and understood'.

I wonder who Roger is . . .

A global success!

The Boeing 737 airliner, introduced in 1968, proved enormously successful. The 900 version can carry up to 189 passengers on short-haul flights.

A large part of its success is its flexibility. Boeing's designers and engineers ensured that it could be adapted to make many different versions.

A Boeing 737 belonging to Germany's national airline, Lufthansa

Stacked planes!

Today's airports are huge places employing thousands of staff. Getting planes in and out needs complex organisation – look at the sky above any major international airport and you'll see all the 'stacked' planes. It's annoying if your suitcase gets lost, but there are millions that don't! And what about freight? Without freight and the income generated by shopping, airlines and airports would make much less money.

Most large modern airports are designed as a circular 'hub'. Planes come to it for loading and unloading.

Airport hubs!

This version of Boeing's 747 jumbo jet has upturned winglets at the end of each wing to reduce drag

49

A JUMBO IN THE SKIES

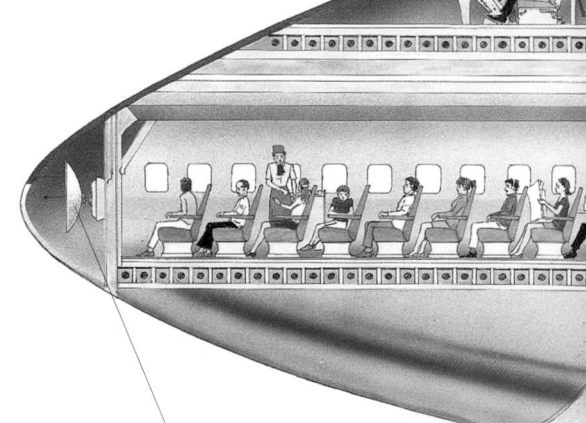

Flight deck

As aircraft became more powerful they could fly above the worst of the weather. This made flying much more comfortable. Competition between airlines increased after World War II, with each promising passengers bigger, faster, and more comfortable planes. Gradually, as more people travelled by air, fares fell. In February 1969, the Boeing 747 was launched. The largest aircraft flying, it could carry 569 passengers and was soon nicknamed the 'jumbo jet'.

Radar dish

Famous Flight

Launch of Boeing 747

Non-stop flights!

The 'jumbo' could fly more than 13,000 kilometres (from London to Honolulu) without refuelling – no other airliner could do that. Within six months of its introduction, more than one million passengers had flown safely on jumbos. After one year, this number had risen to seven million passengers worldwide, with 17 countries operating jumbos.

No wonder they call it 'Jumbo'!

It's enormous!

Fuel burns here

Turbine turned by hot gases drives compressor and fan

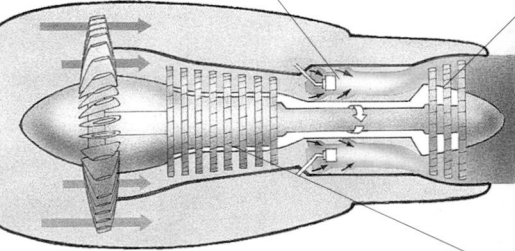

Compressor blows air into combustion chamber

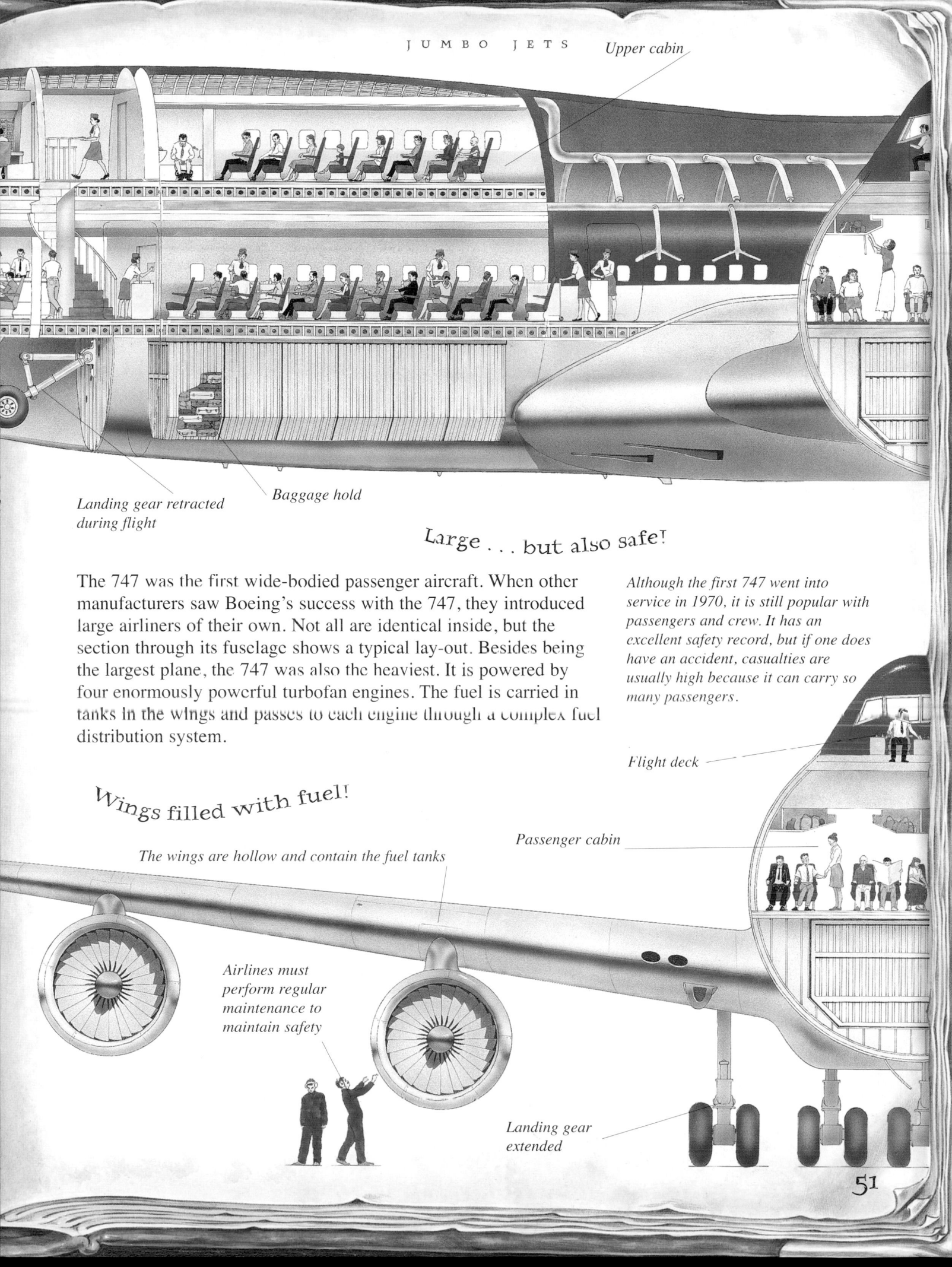

Upper cabin

Landing gear retracted
during flight

Baggage hold

Large . . . but also safe!

The 747 was the first wide-bodied passenger aircraft. When other
manufacturers saw Boeing's success with the 747, they introduced
large airliners of their own. Not all are identical inside, but the
section through its fuselage shows a typical lay-out. Besides being
the largest plane, the 747 was also the heaviest. It is powered by
four enormously powerful turbofan engines. The fuel is carried in
tanks in the wings and passes to each engine through a complex fuel
distribution system.

*Although the first 747 went into
service in 1970, it is still popular with
passengers and crew. It has an
excellent safety record, but if one does
have an accident, casualties are
usually high because it can carry so
many passengers.*

Flight deck

Wings filled with fuel!

Passenger cabin

The wings are hollow and contain the fuel tanks

*Airlines must
perform regular
maintenance to
maintain safety*

*Landing gear
extended*

A SUPERSONIC FUTURE?

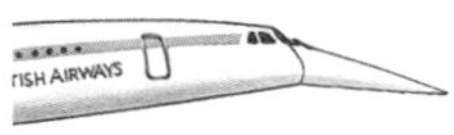

On 2 March 1969, a plane took off that many people believed would be the future for passenger aircraft. The plane was Concorde, the world's first supersonic airliner. An Anglo-French project, the plane flew higher and faster than any other airliner. But, soon after Concorde's launch, the price of fuel oil rose dramatically. This, and the fact that Concorde could only carry about 100 passengers, made it too expensive for most airlines to operate.

Today's airliners have flight decks full of computers, that make Concorde's look very old-fashioned.

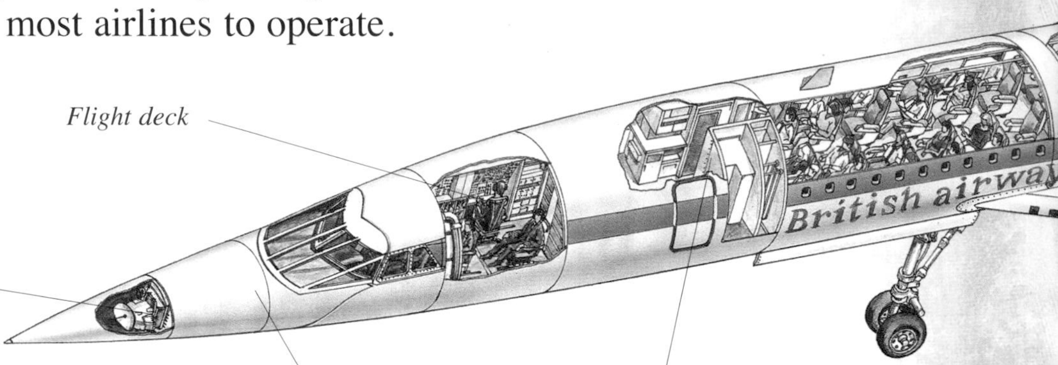

Flight deck

Radar in nose

Nose section

Galley

British airway

Famous Flight

1969

First Concorde Flight

Roaaarrr

Roaaarrr

Squawk!

Sonic booms . . . and crashes!

Concorde was expensive to fly, so fares had to be high. It was most successful on the trans-Atlantic route between Europe and the USA because business executives really could go there and back in one day – flights took about three hours instead of six or seven. British Airways and Air France each had a small fleet of Concordes, but a disastrous crash in 2000 which killed 113 people was something Concorde never recovered from. It was withdrawn from service in 2003. Concerns over noise pollution and the high cost of fuel make it unlikely another supersonic airliner will take to the skies.

A moveable nose!

Concorde's nose section drooped for take-off and landing so the crew could see ahead. It rose when the plane was airborne.

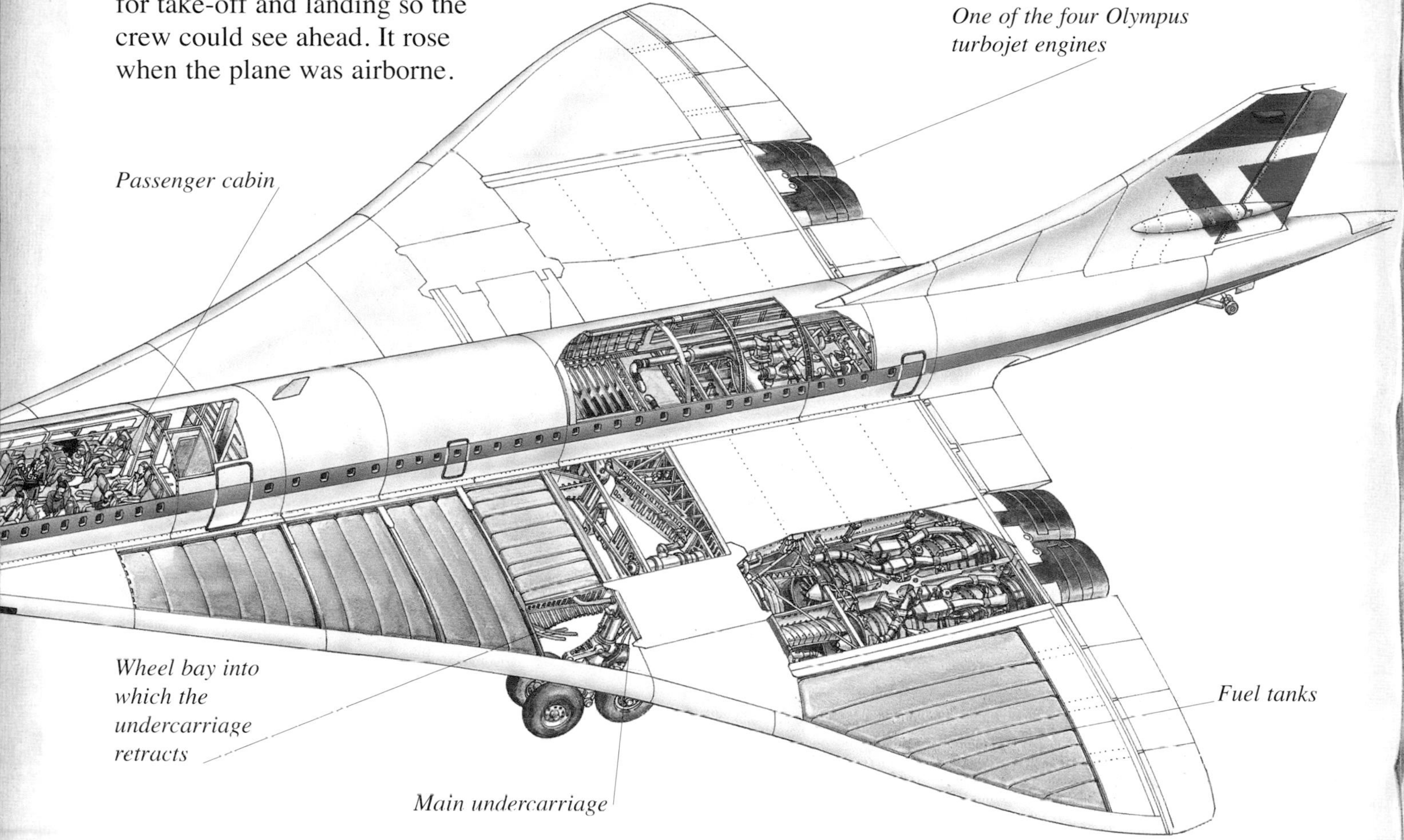

One of the four Olympus turbojet engines
Passenger cabin
Wheel bay into which the undercarriage retracts
Fuel tanks
Main undercarriage

Streamlined!

BRITISH AIRWAYS
G-BOAD

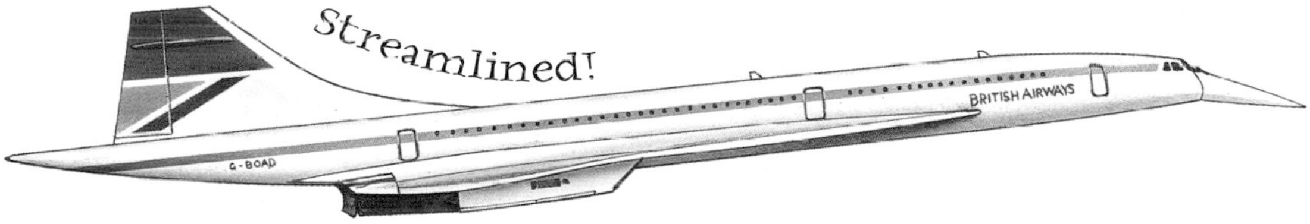

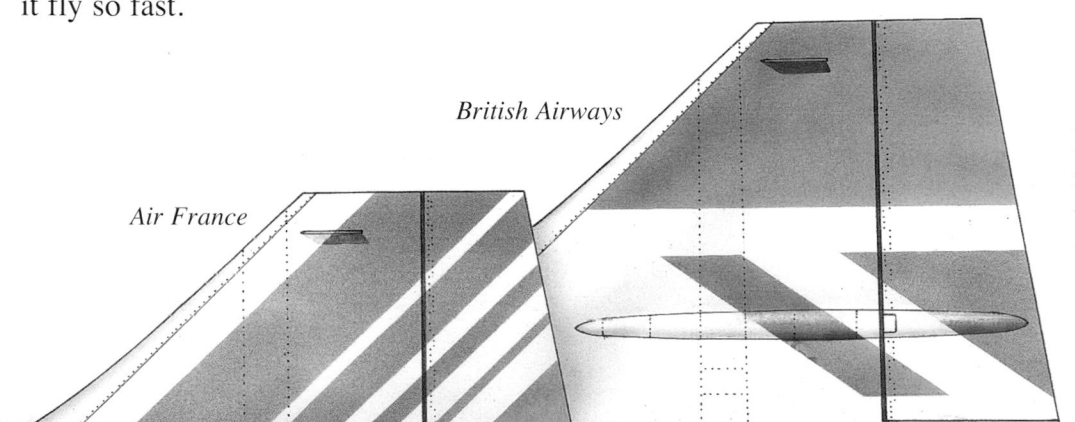

Concorde's slim, streamlined shape was very distinctive. It was this and the two powerful turbojet engines under each wing that helped it fly so fast.

Super expensive!

High prices meant that from the 1970s only two national airlines used Concorde.

British Airways
Air France

FLYING FOR FUN

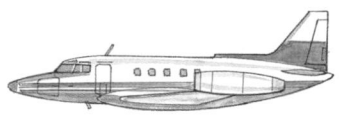

Flying really began because two enthusiastic amateurs were determined to prove that the impossible was possible. It was their hobby. In fact today's huge global aircraft industry really began in a bicycle workshop (pages 12 and 13). For many people flying is still a hobby because of the sense of freedom it gives. But that freedom comes at a cost. Flying for fun is an expensive hobby although, in general, the smaller and lighter the flying machine the cheaper it is to buy and fly – model airplanes are much cheaper!

Safety measure to sport!

Parachuting, originally a safety measure for pilots, is now a popular sport. Steerable chutes help competitors make accurate landings.

Famous Flyer
The Pitts Special
Aerobatic biplane 1944-Present day

Lucky I'm strapped in tightly!

World record!

In 1993, British paraglider Robbie Whittall ascended to 4,526 metres, (over half the height of Everest) to break the world record for altitude. He still holds it today.

Stunt planes!

Stunt flying is fun, but it puts great strain on the plane. The Pitts Special biplane was specially built for stunt flying by Curtis Pitts in 1944.

Hang glider pilots are suspended in a sling below the wings

Hang glider pilots run to take-off then leap into a sling. To control the glider they shift their weight.

Large glass areas gives the pilot greater visibility in the Edgley Optica

Tiger Moth

Thermal power!

Flying Tigers!

The Tiger Moth (above) is still a popular hobby aircraft and is also good for aerobatics.

The Edgley Optica's unstreamlined shape (top) seems to break all the rules of aerodynamics, but it was built for observation purposes and not to break speed records.

Gliders (above) have no engines, so need catapulting or towing by plane into the air. Once airborne they glide on 'thermals' – rising air currents.

Passenger cabin

Flight steps fold down

Twin engines

Business excutives can no longer cross the Atlantic supersonically (pages 53 and 54), but for many, an executive jet is the next best thing.

The 1966 Rockwell Sabreliner (above) was one of the first business jets. They were designed as fully equipped offices in the air.

Travel in luxury on a private jet!

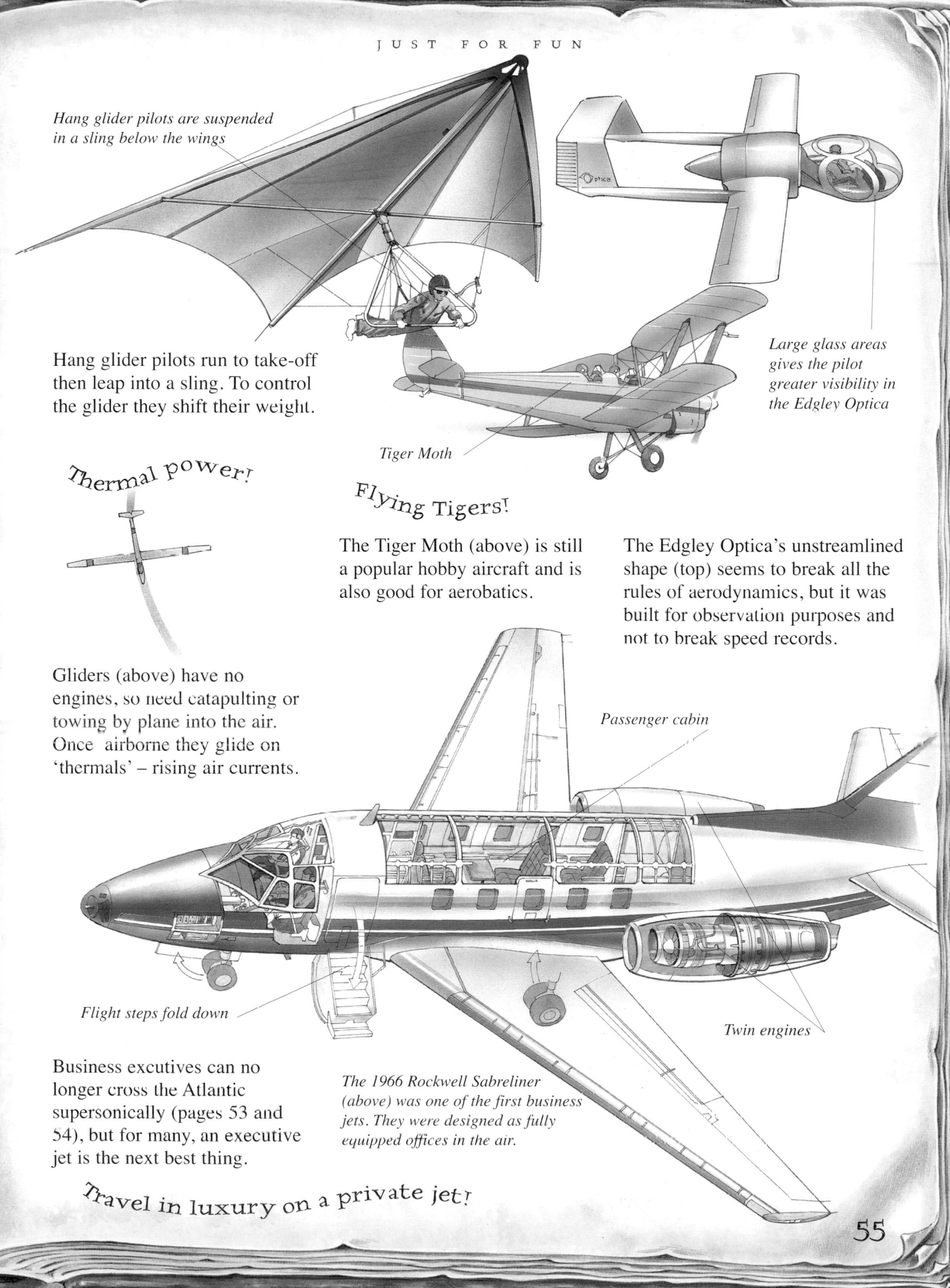

RECORD BREAKERS

Once the Wrights proved flying was possible, others have set some amazing records. One was Bryan Allen (left), an American cyclist who made the first human-powered crossing of the English Channel in 1979. How? He pedalled! His plane, *Gossamer Albatross*, weighed less than he did and he kept it airborne for 2 hours 49 minutes, long enough to make the crossing and enter the record books.

Pedal Power!

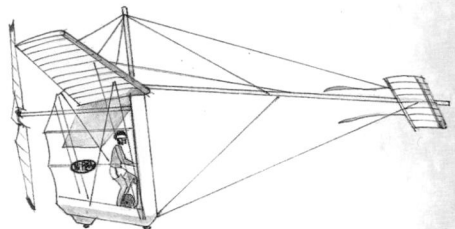

Bryan Allen flew his first plane, Gossamer Condor, *(above) for just over seven minutes in 1977.*

Famous Flight
First Human-Powered Aircraft
1977

Whizzzz

NASA

Puff, Pant!

Whirrr

The Gossamer Condor *had to complete a special course in the shape of a figure eight and travelled a total of 2.17 km from takeoff to landing, at speeds between 16 and 17 km/h. Dr Paul MaCready built on the design of this craft to make* Gossamer Albatross, *which went on to cross the English Channel in 1979.*

Flying fuel tank!

Voyager (above) has a wingspan of 34 metres. It took off for its round-the-world flight from California, returning just over nine days later. The specially designed plane was really just a huge flying fuel tank. It is now on display in the National Air and Space Museum in the US.

Smallest!

ZOOOOOOM

Silver Bullet (above) is the smallest jet to have flown. It was built by American aviator Bob Bishop and has a wingspan of 5.2 metres. Although small, it can still reach a speed of 483 km/h.

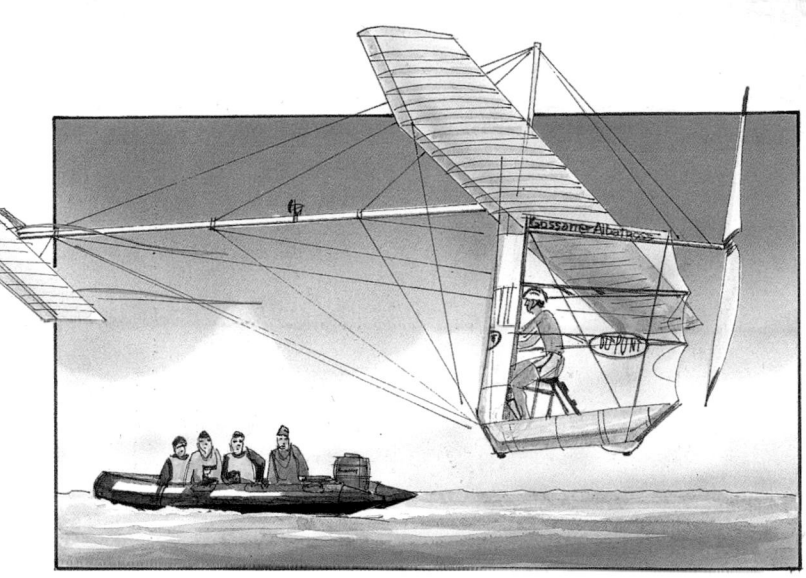

Gossamer Albatross (above) was also specially designed. Like *Gossamer Condor* it was extremely light and designed by engineer Dr Paul MacCready.

World record!

SWOOOOSh

In 2001, Austrian Manfred Ruhmer flew his hang-glider a record-breaking distance of 700.6 km.

In 1988, Greek cyclist Kanellos Kanellopoulos reenacted the legend of Daedalus and Icarus (page 5). His pedal-powered machine Daedalus *was barely five metres above the sea (left).*

Daedalus

Balloons!

In 1987, Richard Branson and Per Linstrand made the first hot-air balloon crossing of the Atlantic – it had only been crossed previously in a helium/gas filled balloon. They flew 1,448 km in just 33 hours. In 1991 they went on to set the Pacific record.

THE FINAL FRONTIER?

Would anyone have imagined in 1903 that *Flyer's* flight of 36 metres could eventually lead to the moon? Probably not, but it did. The 'race to the moon' of the 1950s and 1960s between the USSR and the USA was enormously expensive for both countries. Since then, most space exploration has become a joint venture between countries.

The cost of space travel needed to reduce if there was to be any future for it. The space shuttle *Columbia*, the first reusable spacecraft, was launched in 1981. It was 37 metres long with a wingspan of 24 metres. The shuttle reached 28,000 km/h and orbited at 643 km above Earth.

Famous Flight

First space shuttle launched 1981

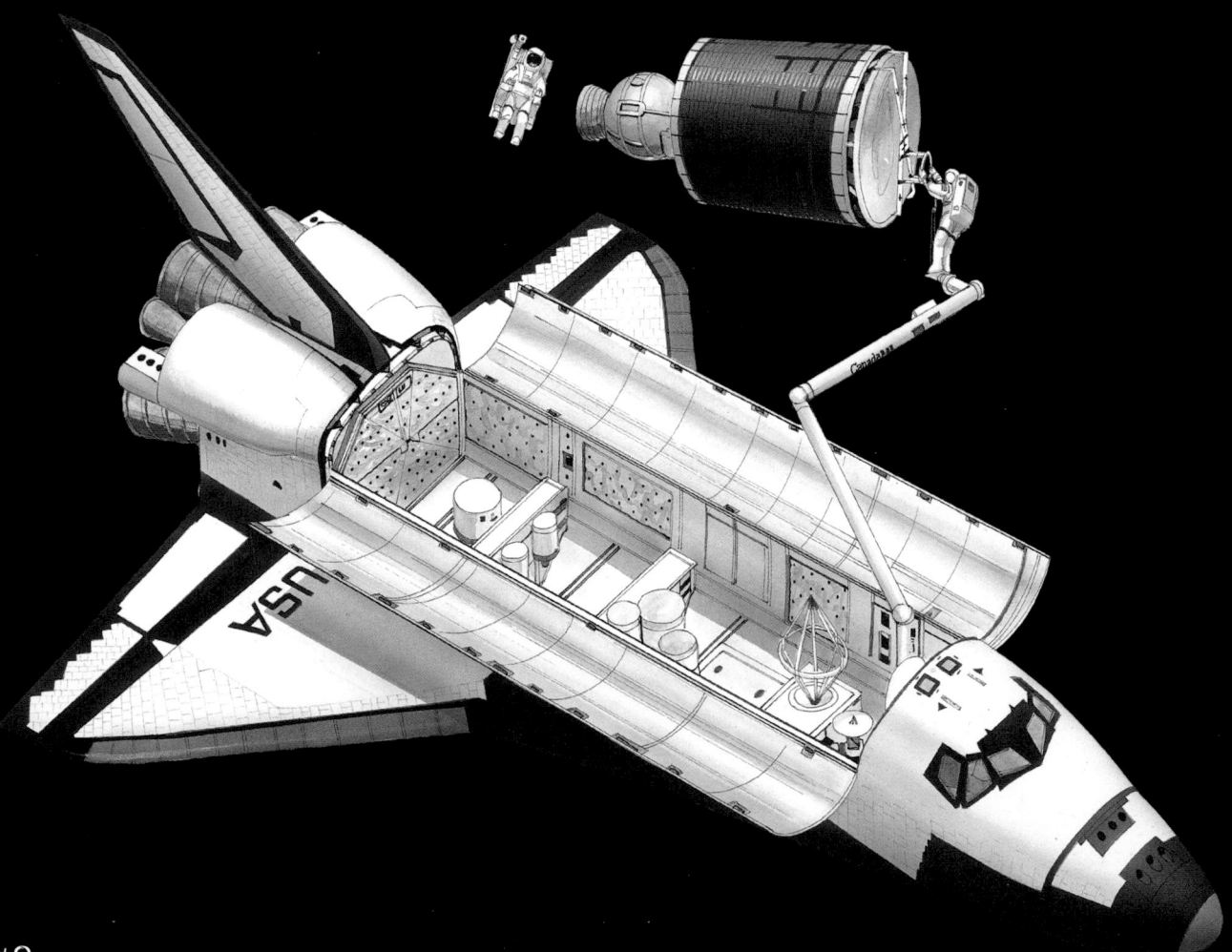

Space stations!

The International Space Station (ISS) was designed as a co-operative effort between 16 countries including the European Space Agency, Russia, Japan and America. Launched on 20 November 1998 and orbiting 354 km above Earth, it was intended to carry a crew of seven and weigh around 450 tonnes when completed. However due to rising costs and delays in construction, the future is uncertain for the ISS. After the tragic loss of *Columbia* in February 2003, NASA stopped all US space shuttle flights and all transport to and from the ISS was by the Russian Soyuz spacecraft.

The ISS has been manned by a crew of at least two astronauts and provided a permanent human presence in space since 2002.

The picture above shows the stages of a shuttle flight. The shuttle takes off strapped to a fuel tank which is jettisoned when empty. Returning to Earth, the shuttle glides down.

Space tourists!

On 21 June 2004, Space Ship One (below right) and its launch craft, *White Knight* made the first privately-funded space flight. *White Knight* carried Space Ship One up to 15,2 km where SS1 detached, fired its engines and reached a height of 100 km above Earth at speeds of Mach 3. In October 2004, the same team won the $10 million Ansari X prize for their achievements.

Modelled on the design of SS1, Virgin Galactic are currently working on a means of developing the business of space tourism. Unfortunately, as with early airlines, ticket costs will initially be very high at $200,000 per seat.

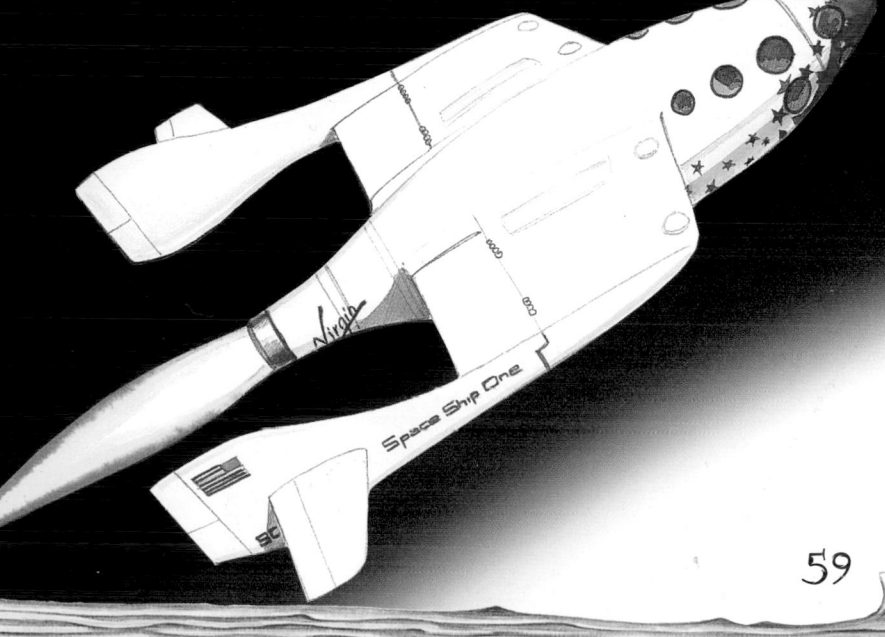

FLYING INTO THE FUTURE

THE FUTURE OF FLIGHT?

Modern computers did not exist when *Flyer* flew for those 12 historic seconds in 1903. Today computers fly aircraft, and pilots often only oversee take-off and landing, although they are there to handle any crisis. In dangerous areas such as war zones, air forces use computer-controlled pilotless aircraft, because although modern aircraft are extremely expensive, the cost of training pilots is even greater. Computers are now essential even before a new type of plane is built. Special programmes test new designs 'in-flight' before the prototype is built. Now pilots train in 'video game' style simulators as well as the cockpit.

Super jumbos!

Airbus, the manufacturer of the new 'super jumbo' was formed after the merger of several European aircraft manufacturers from the UK, Germany, France and Spain. Parts of the giant aircraft have been made in each of these countries and then assembled. It can carry 555 passengers and has a flying range of 15,000 km.

Famous Flight

Airbus takes off!

2005

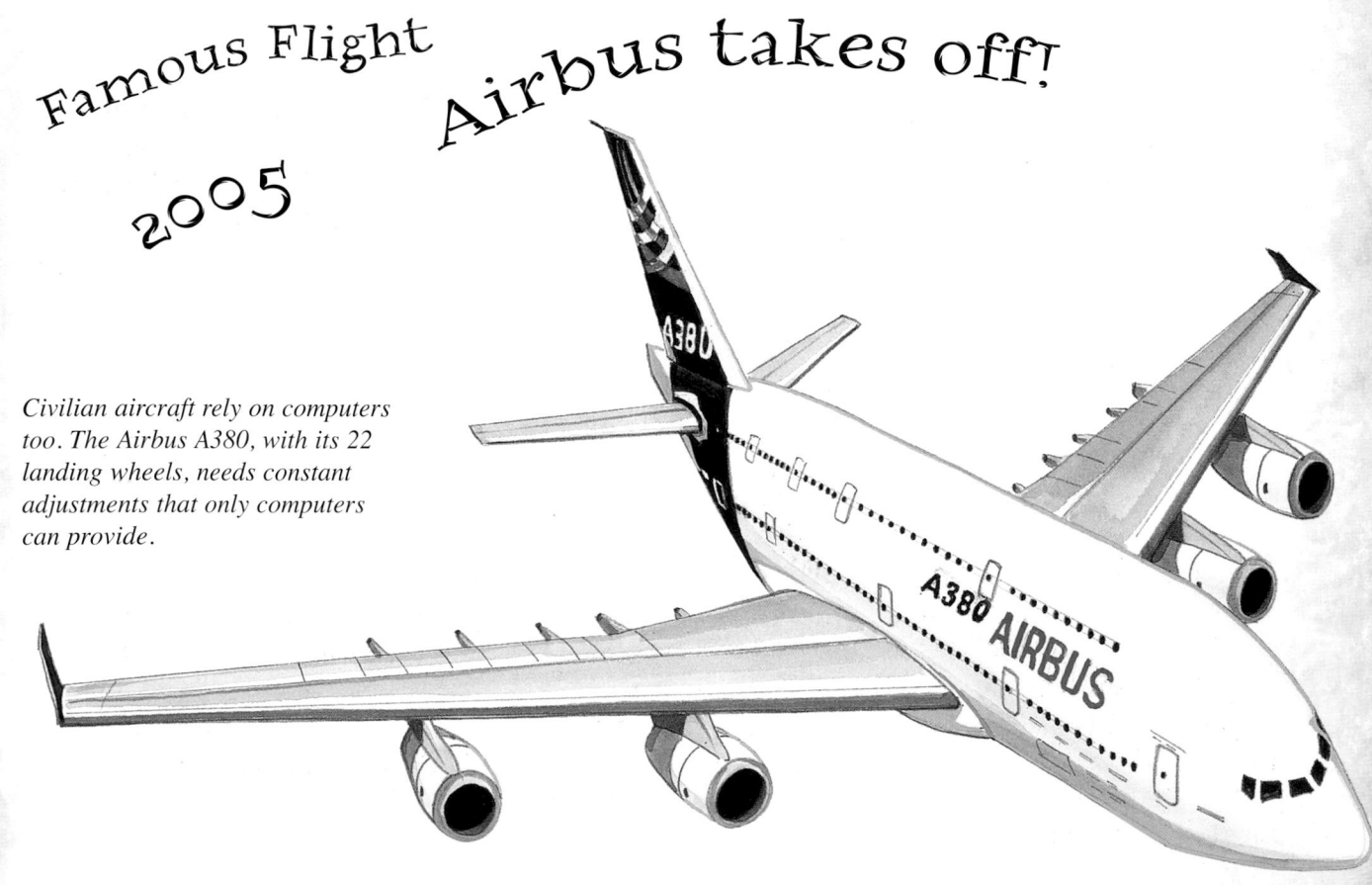

Civilian aircraft rely on computers too. The Airbus A380, with its 22 landing wheels, needs constant adjustments that only computers can provide.

Computer controlled craft!

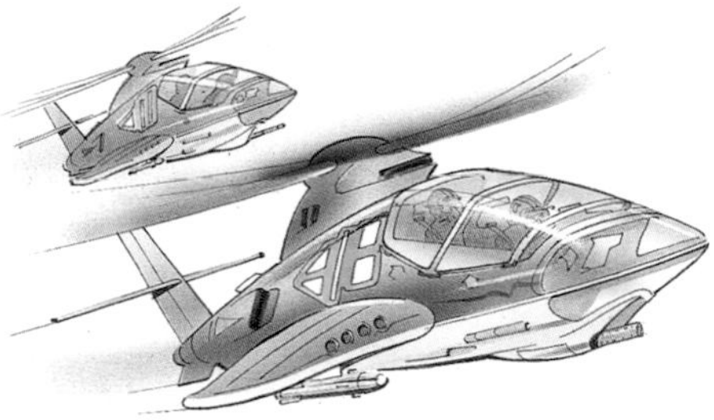

Computers control the combat helicopters (left) designed by Bell/McDonnell Douglas.

Tiltrotor machines (page 60 far left) allow a vertical take-off while enabling much higher speeds than an ordinary helicopter is capable of. Once airborne, the propellers tilt forward making the aircraft move more like a plane.

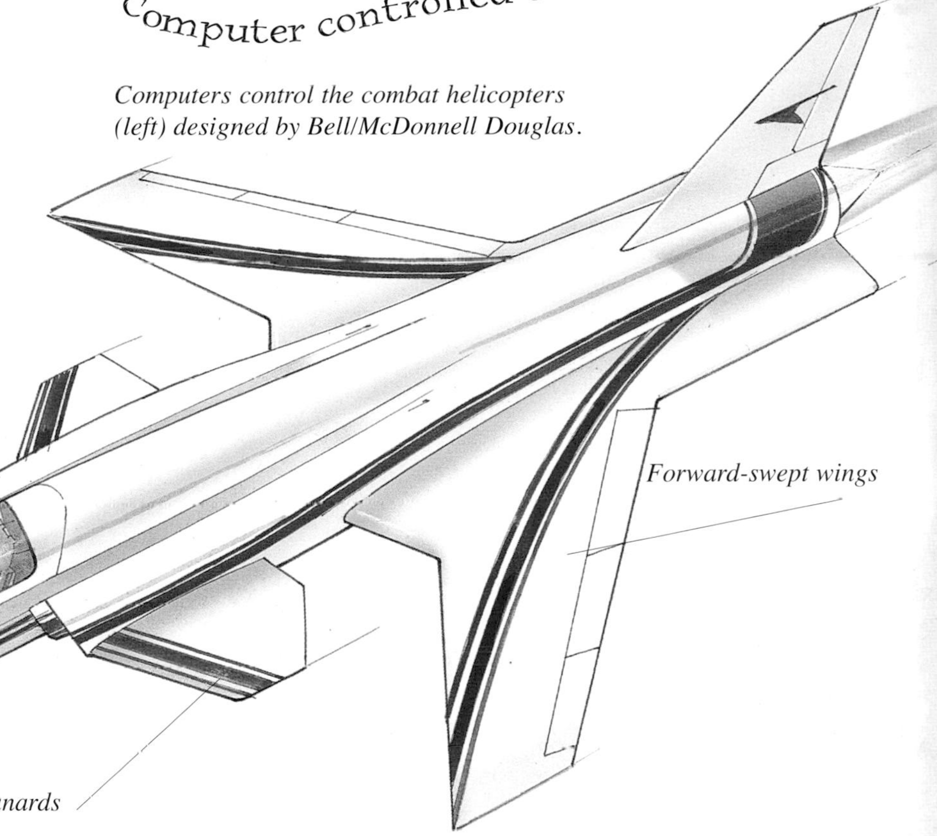

Forward-swept wings

Canards

Look, aim and fire!

Invented in 2004, this interactive helmet allows fighter pilots to lock on and fire at an enemy in the blink of an eye.

The experimental Grumman's X-29 (above) is so unstable at low speeds it needs five on-board computers to help the pilot.

Forward-swept wings make planes agile but unstable. The stubby 'wings' just behind the pilot are called canards.

Solar powered!

Flying creates a great deal of air pollution. As worries increase about pollution and climate change, scientists are searching for alternative fuels. *Pathfinder* (above), first launched in 1995, is a solar-powered wing. It is still at the experimental phase, but who knows what the future holds for it? Perhaps this is the basis of future solar-powered aircraft.

Glossary

altitude height at which aircraft fly. Most airliners fly at about 9,000 metres.

autogyro aircraft halfway between a helicopter and fixed-wing plane. They need a short run along the ground to take off.

aviator another word for pilot. A female aviator is an aviatrix.

biplane airplane with two pairs of wings, one above the other.

canards horizontal stabilisers mounted on the fuselage in front of the wings.

G-force unit of measurement for gravity.

glider unpowered aircraft which gets its lift from rising air currents.

interrupter gear mechanism used in World War I planes. It timed forward-facing machine guns so the bullets passed between the blades of the spinning propeller rather than smashing into them.

jet engine aircraft engine which forces a stream of hot gases out through an opening at the rear of the engine.

lift upward-acting force which stops an aircraft falling.

Mach number way of expressing the speed of sound. Mach 1 equals the speed of sound, Mach 2 is twice the speed of sound, and so on.

monoplane airplane with a single pair of wings.

pod smoothly shaped section into which an aircraft part fits. Most pods are designed for engines.

radar **ra**dio **d**etection **a**nd **r**anging system for detecting the presence, direction, distance and speed of objects.

retractable undercarriage landing legs and wheels of an aircraft which fold away during flight.

rotor blades of a helicopter which rotate (turn).

scramjet **s**upersonic **c**ombustion **ramjet.** Combustion takes place within a stream of supersonic air so it works more like a rocket than a conventional jet engine.

sound barrier approaching the speed of sound, aircraft become more difficult to control as drag increases. It was once believed that aircraft would disintegrate if they broke the sound barrier (went faster than sound).

supersonic faster than the speed of sound. At sea level this is 1227 km/h, at high altitudes it is 1062 km/h.

swept-back wings a design allowing the position of a plane's wings to be moved back so they can reach higher speeds. No longer popular because it decreases efficiency.

thermal rising current of warm air. Used by glider pilots to gain height.

thrust force which drives an aircraft forward through the air.

triplane airplane with three pairs of wings.

turbine blades mounted on an axle. When gas or liquid flow through the blades the axle turns. Turbines are used in jet engines.

turbofan jet engine with a fan in the front to suck air into the engine. Most modern jet aircraft use turbofan engines.

turboprop engine which combined a propeller and a jet engine. Few turboprops are used now and most modern jets have turbofan engines.

USSR (Union of Soviet Socialist Republics) communist states, once ruled as a single state with Moscow as the capital city.

Index

Published in Great Britain in 2006 by
Book House, an imprint of
The Salariya Book Company Ltd
25 Marlborough Place, Brighton BN1 1UB

Please visit the Salariya Book Company at:
www.salariya.com for free electronic versions of:

You Wouldn't Want to Be a Roman Gladiator!
You Wouldn't Want to Be an Egyptian Mummy!
Avoid joining Shackleton's Polar Expedition!

HB ISBN-10: 1-905087-87-X
HB ISBN-13: 978-1-905087-87-7
PB ISBN-10: 1-905087-88-8
PB ISBN-13: 978-1-905087-88-4

Editor: Sophie Izod
Editorial Assistant: Mark Williams
Illustrated by: David Antram, Mark Peppé, John James, Mark Bergin, Carolyn Scrace